DR. SCHWEITZER

of LAMBARÉNÉ

D1595566

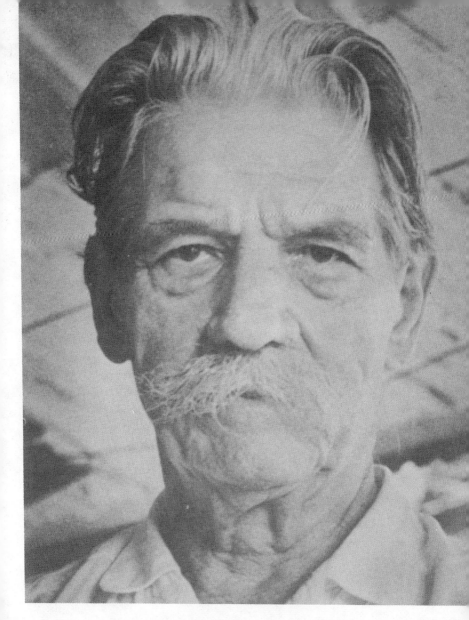

"It is good to be reminded now and then that even in a world struggling with the mome[n] issue of war and peace the individual has problems."

DR. SCHWEITZER

of LAMBARÉNÉ

by Norman Cousins

With Photographs by Clara Urquhart

GREENWOOD PRESS, PUBLISHERS
WESTPORT, CONNECTICUT

Library of Congress Cataloging in Publication Data

Cousins, Norman.
    Dr. Schweitzer of Lambaréné.

    Reprint of the ed. published by Harper, New York.
    1. Schweitzer, Albert, 1875-1965. I. Title.
[CT1098.S45C6 1973]   266'.025'092'4 [B]   73-7075
ISBN 0-8371-6902-X

Originally published in 1960 by Harper & Brothers,
New York

Reprinted with the permission of Harper & Row,
Publishers, Inc.

Reprinted by Greenwood Press, Inc.

First Greenwood reprinting 1973
Second Greenwood reprinting 1977

Library of Congress catalog card number 73-7075

ISBN 0-8371-6902-X

Printed in the United States of America

To My Father

Author's Note

This book is in the nature of a personal appreciation. It does not seek to be either an historical analysis of an eminent contemporary or a detailed biographical treatment. It is concerned with the carrying power of a symbol and with some of the people who are part of it. It was constructed from notes taken on a trip to Africa. Though most of these notes are about a man at Lambaréné, some of them are in the nature of digression. Lambaréné is a good place for digressions, especially those of a retrospective turn.

A word about the photographs. The initials C.U. belong to Clara Urquhart. Mrs. Urquhart is not to be taxed with the responsibility for the photographs that carry no initials; these were taken by the author.

Mrs. Urquhart, who was with me in Lambaréné, has given me the benefit of her own recollections and has made important suggestions about the manuscript. Erica Anderson, who made the major film about Dr. Schweitzer, checked the facts in this manuscript and spared me the agony of a number of errors. Nicholas Balint helped check the proofs. Sallie Lou Parker picked up after me graciously and generously, and put up with an author whose changes on manuscript necessitated at least a dozen retypings. To all these, and to a forbearing wife and daughters, I give acknowledgments and thanks.

N.C.

I

AT THE END of dinner each evening at his jungle Hospital in Lambaréné, French Equatorial Africa, Dr. Albert Schweitzer would fold his napkin, announce the number of the hymn to be sung, get up and walk over to the upright piano on the other side of the room. He would arrange the hymn carefully on the music stand, study it for a moment, then start to play.

I doubt whether I shall ever forget my shock and disbelief when, the first evening of my visit, I saw him approach the upright. Earlier in the day, while exploring the Hospital on my own, I had wandered into the dining room where Dr. Schweitzer and his staff of fifteen eat each day. The first thing that caught my eye was the piano. It must have been at least fifty years old. The keyboard was badly stained; large double screws fastened the ivory to each note. I tried to play but drew back almost instantly. The volume pedal was stuck and the reverberations of the harsh sounds hung in the air. One or more strings were missing on at least a dozen keys. The felt covering the hammers was worn thin and produced pinging effects.

Before coming to Lambaréné, I had heard that under equatorial conditions of extreme heat and moisture one doesn't even try to keep a piano in tune; you make your peace with the inevitable and do the best you can.

Even so, when I saw Dr. Schweitzer sit down at the piano and prop up the hymnbook, I winced. Here was one of history's greatest interpreters of Bach, a man who could fill any concert hall in the world. The best grand piano ever made would be none too good for him. But he was now about to play a dilapidated upright virtually beyond repair. And he went at it easily and with the dignity that never leaves him.

I knew then that I would never be able to put out of my mind the image—painful in one sense, exalting in another—of Schweitzer at the old upright in Lambaréné. For here was the symbol, visible and complete, of everything he had given up in order to found a hospital in Africa. Renunciation by itself may mean little. What is renounced and the purpose of the renunciation—that is what is important. In the case of Albert Schweitzer, renunciation involved a distinguished career as organist and pianist; it extended to the intimate study and analysis of the nature of music in general and the organ in particular; it embraced a detailed understanding of the life and meaning of Johann Sebastian Bach. In all of this work there was the meticulous pursuit of perfection. Yet this did not exhaust the renunciation. There was a record in theology, philosophy, and history, in each of which Schweitzer had made major contributions as teacher and author. Solid foundations had been built for a lifelong career in any of these fields.

I wrote a moment ago that I felt not only pain but a certain inspiration in the image of Schweitzer at the old piano. For the amazing and wondrous thing was that the piano seemed to lose its poverty in his hands. Whatever its capacity was to yield music was now being fully realized. The tinniness and chattering echoes seemed subdued. It may be that this was the result of Schweitzer's intimate acquaintance with the piano, enabling him to avoid the rebellious keys and favoring only the co-operative ones. Whatever the reason, his being at the piano strangely seemed to make it right.

And, in a curious way, I discovered that this was to be true of almost everything else at Lambaréné. Schweitzer's being there made it right. Much of what you saw for the first time at the Hospital seemed so primitive and inadequate as to startle. But when Dr. Schweitzer walked through the grounds, everything seemed as it should be. More than that: the profound meaning of Lambaréné suddenly came to life. And I was to learn that there was a reason behind everything at Lambaréné.

And I was to get close to one of the things that drew me to Lambaréné—not Schweitzer's purpose, which was clear enough, but the sources of that purpose, about which I had long wondered.

"YOU MUST COME to Lambaréné," Emory Ross had said early in 1955. "There is something there that I can't capture for you in words but it will mean much to you when you come near it."

Emory Ross was the head of the Schweitzer Fellowship in the United States. He was a former missionary who was now devoting his life to advancing the cause of the African people. He had helped to build schools in various parts of Africa; he had brought promising African students to American colleges and universities; he had raised thousands of dollars for Dr. Schweitzer's Hospital in Lambaréné.

After being with Emory Ross for only a minute or two, you felt you were with a country doctor whose knowledge and skill could put him at the head of almost any hospital in the country but who preferred to sit at the non-specialized bedsides of people who needed him. Emory Ross's manner was extraordinarily kind and reassuring; you never left him with the feeling that half of what you wanted to talk to him about had been left unsaid.

One of the things Emory Ross and I had discusssed at those early meetings was Dr. Schweitzer's unfinished literary works. There were at least two books on which he had been working off and on for more than a quarter of a century. One was concerned with philosophy and history; the other with theology.

Dr. Ross said he believed the manuscripts were fairly close to completion, but that the Hospital's demands on Schweitzer's time were increasing with each passing year. So far as Dr. Ross knew, months would go by without the Doctor's being able to touch his manuscripts. Worse still was the fact that there were no carbon copies. The Doctor wrote in longhand on faded sheets of paper. He was in the habit of hanging them on nails in his room; Dr. Ross spoke of the hazards of moisture, wandering goats, possible fire, and just plain loss.

"I tremble when I think of what would happen if some of that manuscript should come undone," he said.

We discussed various means of persuading the Doctor, then in his eighty-first year, both to take the time necessary to finish his books and to provide for the safety of the manuscripts. We also considered various methods for making duplicate copies, and we agreed to investigate the comparative merits of microfilming, duplicating machines, and plain photography. None of these devices, of course, could be used without the permission and co-operation of the Doctor himself. And here we anticipated trouble. Emory Ross emphasized that Dr. Schweitzer was a perfectionist who was severely reluctant to part with anything he wrote that was not absolutely final and complete. Dr. Ross was contemplating a trip to Lambaréné, but he said he didn't feel in a position to press the issue.

"It's too easy for the Doctor to say 'no' to me. You've got to come and put it to him. It won't be easy. If his mind is made up about something, it takes some real powers of persuasion to move him. Even if we don't succeed, it is important that you come. It will be an experience you'll never forget."

I could feel the beginning of an irresistible tug; but I had only recently returned from Japan in connection with the project to provide reconstructive surgery for some young women from Hiroshima who had been disfigured by the atomic bombing, and my time away from the magazine was limited. And so I told Dr. Ross that much as I wanted to go, I couldn't quite be sure I could do so.

In the weeks that followed, Dr. Ross and I met with other members of the Schweitzer Fellowship. I recall with particular pleasure a luncheon with Erica Anderson, Jerome Hill, and Eugene Exman. Miss Anderson had just returned from Lambaréné where she worked on a film biography of Dr. Schweitzer. Miss Anderson had also just completed, in collaboration with Eugene Exman, vice-president of Harper & Brothers, a picture-and-text book about Dr. Schweitzer and the Hospital.

Emory Ross explained the purpose of the luncheon to the small group. He spoke of the invaluable literary treasures now at Lambaréné and the loss to the world if they should be damaged or lost.

Then he asked: "What do you think the chances are that we could persuade the Doctor to have the manuscripts duplicated?"

"I can tell you," Miss Anderson said, "that the Doctor is suspicious of anyone who arrives at Lambaréné with a lot of mechanical equipment."

"If you approach the Doctor about it directly, it's my guess he'd give you a flat 'no,' " Eugene Exman said. "He just doesn't like to be prodded about his manuscripts—either with respect to finishing them or taking precautions for their physical safety. You've got to give this real thought."

Jerome Hill nodded assent.

As I listened, a picture formed in my mind of Schweitzer as an austere and remote figure who could be approached only with the greatest care. I found it interesting that even those who knew him best had to conjecture about his response to situations. They had to plan any action involving him as carefully as they would the strategy for a military campaign.

"Perhaps we ought also to find out what Dr. Schweitzer's friends in Europe think," Dr. Ross said. "I am sure Emil Mettler in London would know something about the manuscripts. And Dr. Schweitzer's daughter in Zurich ought to know something about it. J. D. Newth in London, who is Dr. Schweitzer's English publisher, may be able to give us a lead."

Erica Anderson's eyes were sparkling with the challenge.

"I think maybe the best thing to do would be just to go there," she said. "After you are there a while, tell the Doctor what you want to do. But just don't turn up with a lot of equipment showing. I made the mistake of doing that once and I ought to know."

I recalled that several years earlier Erica Anderson had received a flat refusal from Dr. Schweitzer when she wrote to him about her hope that she might do a film story of his life. But he invited her to come to Lambaréné just the same—without the film equipment. She went and got him to change his mind.

Incidents were then related at the table that gave me a contrasting picture of the Doctor to the one I had had earlier. I had associated him with warmth and responsiveness. The new image seemed somewhat aloof and austere. And a paradox began to emerge. Later, I was to learn at Lambaréné, that this was only one of several paradoxes about the man whose life embraced at least four full careers.

THE RECEPTIONIST at *The Saturday Review* announced Mr. Newth from London, representing A. & C. Black, publishers. He said he was on a short visit to the United States and had learned from Emory Ross of the prospect of our trip to Lambaréné.

I told Mr. Newth, as I had earlier told Emory Ross, that eager as I was to go, the matter was far from settled. I explained the circumstances that were holding me back.

"We are still hopeful that we can publish the Schweitzer manuscripts during his lifetime," he said. "I don't want to prod, but it might be helpful if you could manage the trip. A new voice is needed to talk to the Doctor. He has heard the same arguments from his old friends for so many years that it is too easy for him to wave them aside. We need fresh reinforcements. I hope you will do it."

What Mr. Newth said was most persuasive; I thanked him and told him I would keep the matter open. As the weeks passed, however, my reluctance to leave the family and the magazine so soon after the Far East trip became strengthened. Besides, the project for the Hiroshima Maidens was now in full swing, with dozens of operations yet to be performed by Dr. Arthur Barsky, Dr. Bernard Simon, and Dr. Sidney Kahn. The medical program, too, under Dr. William Hitzig, was far from complete.

When the time neared for Dr. Ross's own trip to Lambaréné, he spoke to me again about the possibility of my accompanying him. The chances were now nil. But he exacted a promise that I would go when I could. Dr. Ross would take no photographing equipment with him but would attempt to clear the way for my visit when I could make it. Meanwhile, I was to write to Dr. Schweitzer, urging him to give favorable consideration to our project.

Several weeks later, a reply arrived from Lambaréné. The Doctor was most cordial and thanked me for my interest, but said that he just did not have enough time to do anything about the manuscripts. He invited me to visit him at the Hospital when I felt free to do so. A postscript referred to an editorial I had written some time earlier, called "The Point about Schweitzer." In that editorial I had differed with recent visitors to Lambaréné who had complained about the primitive aspects of the place. The point I tried to make was that the Schweitzer symbol was more important than modern facilities. Dr. Schweitzer's postscript said that he hoped to justify the kind things I had written about him.

When Emory Ross returned from Africa several months later, he brought back a report of cautious optimism. The Doctor didn't seem to want to talk about his manuscripts at first. But Dr. Ross managed to find him alone one afternoon and spoke to him fully about the concerns of his friends. Dr. Schweitzer's response enabled Emory Ross to come away with the feeling that the project now had an even chance at least.

By this time, the surgical program of the Hiroshima Maidens was well advanced. Nine of the girls had completed all their operations and would soon be ready to return to their families in Japan. The others would probably be ready to return as a group in the fall. My obligations were thinning out.

ONE DAY IN September, 1956, Mrs. Clara Urquhart, who had been associated with Dr. Schweitzer for many years and who had just come from Lambaréné, visited the offices of the magazine. She had much to relate about Schweitzer—about his work and manuscripts and, in general, about his state of mind. She had been with the Doctor at the time he read my letter concerning his books, and she had something to say in that connection.

"You must not be discouraged," she began.

Later, I was to discover that no five words were more characteristic of Clara Urquhart than "you must not be discouraged." She never underestimated the difficult but never made the mistake, either, of confusing the difficult with the impossible.

"You must not be discouraged," she said again, "just because the Doctor said 'no' to you in his letter. He is so overburdened with work at the Hospital that he almost automatically says 'no' to anything that would make additional demands on his time. A certain innate modesty often makes him seem negative. But I think he really wants to complete his books."

"Has he done any work on them recently?"

"Very little, if at all. I've been after him for years about it."

"Can anything be done? Should anything be done?"

"Recently," she said, "he promised me he would do some work on the manuscripts. He came to his room early in the afternoon and began to write. I returned an hour later and peeked into the room. The Doctor was no longer there. A breeze had blown some of the sheets of the manuscripts off the desk. An antelope had wandered into the room. Some of the sheets had been trampled upon. I had no way of knowing whether any had been eaten.

"I gathered up the papers and smoothed them out. Right then, I became determined to see this through.

"When the Doctor returned to the room I told him what had happened. He shrugged. I said that even though he was reluctant to finish the manuscripts, the least he could do was to attend to the physical safety of his papers.

"Unlike previous occasions, when he brushed that kind of talk aside, this time he said nothing. My guess is that he is about ready to change his mind. I hope you will accept his invitation to come to Lambaréné. And so, if you want an accomplice in the project to copy the manuscript, I'd like to volunteer."

You didn't have to be with Clara Urquhart very long to know that this slight, dark woman possessed a rare combination of intensity of feeling with calmness of manner. She knew how to establish rapport in ten minutes that would take some people ten weeks. Also, she had the art of absolute relevance. When she listened, you had the feeling that all her energy was being mobilized in absorbing every sound and capturing your total intent. And when she spoke, she would address herself with precision to your questions or the things that interested you—and frequently to the thought behind your questions.

She had brought with her some photographs she had taken at Lambaréné over the years. Many of them were being incorporated in a book about Schweitzer shortly to be issued in London. Several of the photographs were intimate portraits of Dr. Schweitzer. They showed a face of vast power and purpose. It was lean and strong, with lines associated with expressiveness and sensitivity rather than with age. The eyes were set wide apart; they were like steel lanterns in the rugged landscape of his face.

Other photographs were of the people associated with Schweitzer at the Hospital. These were people I wanted to meet, and I said so.

"When are you leaving for Lambaréné?" Clara Urquhart asked.

I said I thought very soon.

THERE WAS YET another reason why I felt compelled to go to Lambaréné.

Ever since the end of the war, there had been one voice which might have had a powerful effect on the biggest issue of the age, but that voice was silent. I knew that Albert Schweitzer had deliberately avoided political issues in order to confine himself to the fundamental and overriding moral questions of concern to the entire human community. But such an overriding question now existed. It was whether the conditions which made human life possible on this planet could be maintained. The means now existed that could alter or destroy those conditions.

Could anyone who was concerned about the problem of ethics in modern man exempt himself from such a question? Albert Schweitzer believed in the sacredness of man. Was there no moral issue if man's genes were to be twisted, if the air he breathed was to be fouled, if unborn generations were to be punished for his present failures?

This crisis could not be easily met by the political leaders of the nations. For the requirements of sovereignty too often came first. The political leader was the spearhead of that total sovereignty, its chief presiding officer. In order that the entire human grouping be served, it would become necessary to create something higher than the nation itself; indeed, it would be necessary to create the means whereby the nation would find security through means other than massive armaments or coalitions. And if something beyond the nation had to be advocated, the national leaders might not be the most logical spokesmen. A man like Albert Schweitzer might enable people to see the need for fashioning allegiances to each other as members of the human commonwealth. What man most lacked was a consciousness of his relationship to other human beings. He lacked adequate awareness of the gift of human life and what was now required to preserve it. Alongside the real threat to life on earth the razor-sharp distinctions he insisted on making between himself and others now served as a dead weight for his hopes.

If I was wrong about the nature of the problem; if I was wrong about the feeling I had that time did not work for us but against us, then the man who could convince me of this was Albert Schweitzer. But if Albert Schweitzer agreed that the problem was real and universal, then it was important and proper for him to speak. And if his reluctance to speak was the result of humility or doubts as to whether his words would be heard, then I could at least attempt to remove these doubts. I did not take lightly the privilege of being in a position to try.

NOW THE REAL planning for the trip began. I had two more meetings with Clara Urquhart before she left for London. She also came out to the house at a picnic for the Hiroshima Maidens and met my wife Ellen and the four girls.

At one of these meetings she had a long checklist of questions to be asked and things to be done.

"How's your French?" she asked. "The Doctor does not speak English though he reads it with little difficulty and understands far more than he admits."

"My French is about the way you describe the Doctor's English."

"What about German?"

"Nil."

"You must not be discouraged," she said. "The Doctor is accustomed to communicating with English-speaking visitors through an interpreter, in German."

When I asked who would do the interpreting, Clara Urquhart said this was all part of the work of the "accomplice's" job that she had volunteered to perform.

Her next question concerned our approximate date of departure.

I made some hasty calculations. The Hiroshima Maidens still in the United States would be returning in October or November. The busy season at the magazine tapered off just before Christmas. That would mean that I might be able to get to Lambaréné late in December or early in January.

Mrs. Urquhart's plan was to leave for London and Rome to see some friends, then to return to her home in Johannesburg for a month. We could meet in Johannesburg, perhaps, she said, then go to Lambaréné. Meanwhile, she would write to Dr. Schweitzer to say that we were definitely coming.

"You'd better make up your mind to stay for a full week or more," she said. "The Doctor says that short visits make him nervous."

I agreed to stay for as long as was required to do the job.

"Now," she said, "comes the most important matter of all. You've got to promise that you won't be disillusioned."

I smiled.

"You mean a hospital ward without bedsheets, lack of sanitation,

and all that sort of thing?" I said. "Please don't let it worry you;
I know all about it. It was this kind of argument that seemed to
me all along to miss the main point about Schweitzer."

"There's something more important than that," she replied. "I'm
talking about Schweitzer himself."

This startled me. "Why is there any danger that I or anyone
else would be disillusioned about Schweitzer?"

"Some people are. They come to Lambaréné with an image of a
sort of sweet saintly St. Francis feeding the birds and they see instead
a driving man fighting the jungle and African lethargy and they do
not remain for a sufficiently long period to see or sense the goodness
and saintliness underneath. They go away feeling hurt and unhappy."

I was touched by her concern but still puzzled. What was there
about Schweitzer that created "hurt and unhappy" feelings in
people? Whatever the answer, I couldn't guarantee Clara Urquhart
what my feelings would be after I met him.

"Of course not," she said. "I just want to be sure you'll stay
long enough to get over some first impressions that may not be so
favorable."

"Such as?"

"Such as the fact that those who do not know the Doctor will
think that his manner toward the indigene or black is unfeeling
and authoritarian.

"Such as the fact that his views seem to reflect little confidence
in the Africans to whom he has given his life. Schweitzer has deeper
and wider dimensions than anyone else I have met. If evaluated
from a superficial viewpoint the image is distorted. For better or for
worse Schweitzer is a patriarch. I remember saying to him that he
was an enlightened despot—to which he replied: 'An enlightened
despot is able to give the greatest amount of freedom.'

"If one fails to remember that his basic motivation is reverence
for life—he might seem arbitrary in his dealings with those around
him. Just wait and observe for the first few days."

Three months later, I was on my way to Lambaréné.

II

THE AIR CONNECTION from Brazzaville to Lambaréné in French Equatorial Africa was probably the most hazardous regularly scheduled flight in the world. It was operated by Air France over jungle mountain country. But the safety record of this particular run was close to the top among the world's airlines.

The men who flew the DC-3 on these jungle hops had earned a high reputation in the society of world airline pilots. The African "airports" at which they stopped had no radio beams for guiding planes through fog and rain, no light towers or signal beacons flashing across the sky, no neon ground markers or flares, no paved landing strips to pick out from the air—just a clearing with a dirt or grass strip. There were no sprawling cities to help a pilot get his bearings, no air terminal buildings or anything approaching them; generally, just a single small structure that served as an open shelter. Jungle country tends to look pretty much alike when you fly north from the Congo. Yet these airmen had a homing-pigeon touch at the controls that was the talk of their trade.

While we were waiting at the Brazzaville airport for the announcement that our plane was ready, Clara Urquhart called out to a tall, slender young man of about thirty who had just walked into the terminal building. She identified him as Dr. Frank Catchpool, from the staff of the Schweitzer Hospital.

Dr. Catchpool was obviously deeply pleased to see her. It developed that she had made the original arrangements with Dr. Schweitzer for Dr. Catchpool to go to Lambaréné. Frank Catchpool was an English citizen and a Quaker who, like many others, had been inspired by Dr. Schweitzer's example. When he first met Clara in London, he inquired about the Hospital and his chances for joining the staff. Clara wrote to Dr. Schweitzer and the matter was arranged.

Now, at the Brazzaville airport, Clara was able to chat with him for the first time since he had been at Lambaréné. We learned that he had been at the Hospital a little more than a month. He had come to Brazzaville five days earlier, he said somewhat ruefully, because of a little dog.

It all began about a week ago, he explained. One of the managers of a nearby French lumber camp had brought his pet dog, breed anonymous, to the hospital. The dog had been suffering for some weeks with a persistent cough. Dr. Schweitzer's Hospital turns away no patients, regardless of color, species, or previous condition of servitude. And so the manager put his dog under Dr. Schweitzer's care. The staff held a consultation; the consensus was that a bone was stuck in his throat. There being no X-ray machines in operation at Lambaréné, the diagnosis could not be confirmed. In any event, it was decided to operate.

Dr. Catchpool, who had had some previous experience, volunteered to apply the anesthetic. He cautioned the other surgeons and nurses about the astounding power in the sudden moves of even a small animal at the time the anesthetic is applied.

His apprehensions were all too accurate. Just as the anesthetic was applied to his mouth, the dog jerked free and bit Dr. Catchpool on the arm. A second attempt was successful, and the small obstruction was removed.

That evening, Dr. Catchpool's arm began to swell and showed discoloration. There being no antirabies serum at the Hospital, Dr. Schweitzer ordered both Dr. Catchpool and the dog to depart immediately for the hospital at Brazzaville, the former to receive antirabies injections, the latter to be put under observation. And now, four days later, both patients were returning to Lambaréné, the doctor having had his shots, and the dog having developed no symptoms of rabies. The dog was now in a crate which was already checked in and waiting to be loaded.

"I wish I could say I didn't feel pretty silly about this whole business," Dr. Catchpool said. "Dr. Schweitzer must have a rather poor opinion of me for having allowed myself to get into this mess. Here I am at the Hospital only a few weeks and I get immobilized by a little dog."

Clara said she was certain that Dr. Schweitzer had only the most sympathetic understanding of the situation.

"That brings up something else," he said. "I'm afraid I don't know where I stand with the Doctor. We've hardly spoken, except for the most routine things. I haven't wanted to go directly to him and tell him about the kind of work I'd like to do at the Hospital or to discuss other things on my mind. I just haven't got the heart to take up a moment of his time.

"You sound discouraged; you mustn't be," Clara said. "You recall that I asked you not to form any judgments until you had been there at least a month. Give yourself a little more time. Many of the things that are troubling you now will fall into place. What kind of work have you been doing at the Hospital?"

Dr. Catchpool grinned.

"I'm the chief electrician and engineer," he said. "I diagnose faulty wiring and operate on sluggish generators."

"I'm sure what you are doing is most essential," Clara said. "Besides, if I may say so, some of this at least is your own fault. You insisted that I say nothing to the Doctor about your excellence as a physician or your very high recommendations. The Doctor is disposed to take people at their own evaluation of themselves. And I'm sure that when you got to Lambaréné, you persisted in underrating yourself. But you must not be discouraged. Your chance will come."

An attendant came over to announce that our plane was ready.

Dr. Catchpool went off to look after the dog. Clara and I collected our hand luggage and boarded the plane. A moment later Dr. Catchpool joined us.

The air distance between Brazzaville and Lambaréné is perhaps no more than four hundred miles on a straight line. But the planes fly a zigzag route in order to cover the various jungle air stations en route to Lambaréné. The flight therefore generally requires from five to six hours. I memorized the colorful names of the jungle towns at which we stopped so I could tell Ellen and the girls about them when I returned—names like Djambala, Mayumba, Tchibanga, Mouila.

At each stop, curious children from surrounding villages would gather near the open shelter close to the landing strip. They would cluster together and stare with open-eyed wonder at the gleaming steel bird. At Tchibanga two children at the edge of the crowd were having a short game of catch with a rubber ball. I walked toward them and made the kind of throwing motion that indicated I wanted to be invited to join in. One of them tossed me the ball. I threw it back, then he smiled broadly and put some muscle into his next pitch.

I looked at the other children. They seemed astonished to observe a white man obviously enjoying himself in a game with black children. Then, suddenly, a clamor went up as at least fifty youngsters called out to join the fun. I would toss the ball into a sea of waving arms and out it would come again. One boy, about twelve or thirteen, sprang high in the air and caught the ball with one hand. Then he ran off at a distance of about forty yards so that he could show me how far he could throw. This in turn set up a cry from at least a dozen others who wanted to do the same. Almost before I knew it, children were streaking all over the airport clearing. It made me think of one of those bull-fighting festivals when the spectators come swarming down into the arena to try their luck with the brave bulls.

The two African policemen stationed at the field seemed agreeable enough when the game of catch had started innocently a few minutes earlier. But now the point of diminishing returns in their good will was just being reached. I beckoned to the youngsters that the game was over, handed the ball to its young owner, and thanked him.

Then I opened my camera and asked my ball-playing companion for the privilege of his photograph. Instead of ending the clamor, this merely set a new stage for it. In a matter of seconds, the crowd closed in on me and pinned me to the spot as each child called out for his right to be photographed.

All this while, Clara and Dr. Catchpool stood on the far side of the crowd, close to the plane. They were enjoying themselves hugely. Clara's expression as much as said: "You got yourself into it; now get yourself out of it."

Finally, the two African policemen made it clear to the youngsters that the big steel bird was ready to go into the sky again, and they helped to detach me from their midst. I doubt whether I shall ever forget the high-pitched deafening yells of *"au revoir"* and the wildly waving arms of the children as I boarded the plane.

"I hope you noticed how the children drew back at first when you approached but how quickly they responded when they saw that you wanted to make friends," Clara said after the plane had leveled off in flight.

It was, I agreed, very striking.

"You will find that this same thing is true of Africans of all ages almost everywhere on the continent," she said. "There is that initial hesitation. They are not sure what you want or intend to do. They are conditioned to react almost chemically against a white skin. But once you make it clear that you approach them as friends, the response is warm and hearty, almost overwhelming."

She paused, and her words seemed to hang in the air for a moment.

"Let me amend that a bit," she said. "I suddenly realize that this is the kind of observation I would have made almost automatically only a few years ago. But it is no longer true; at least, not to the same extent."

"No longer true in what way?" I asked.

"Things are changing in Africa, very fast," she said. "So fast that it becomes necessary to check one's ideas and reactions now and then just to make sure they are up to date. I am not sure that it is as easy now for a friendly white person to gain the good will and confidence of the Africans as it was only a short time ago.

"The atmosphere has changed. It's more tense. The color lines are hardening. More and more Africans are getting caught up in the nationalist movements. Just as many white people have a tendency to make generalizations about the characters and abilities of the blacks, so there is now a tendency by the blacks to make blanket generalizations about all whites. The feeling is growing that all whites are to be feared and opposed. And a white is identified as anyone who stands or appears to stand in the way of their eventual control of their nation.

"But even here, I've got to be careful not to overstate," she continued. "I don't want you to think that Africans don't smile any more or won't be friendly. Of course they will. What I'm trying to do is give you some idea that those of us who have lived in Africa a long time are aware of a tightening in the air. It's like a far-off storm. You continue to do everything you usually do in good weather but there's that uneasy feeling in the back of your mind that you'd better get ready for a sharp change."

AS SHE SPOKE I thought back to my experience involving those "uneasy" feelings a few days earlier in Johannesburg.

In planning my trip to Lambaréné, it had seemed foolish to travel that far without seeing even a little of the Union of South Africa. For distance, these days, is measured not by miles but by hours. And hours are translated into air units. A nonstop air hop is regarded as one unit. For example, in 1956—before the large-scale use of jets—New York to San Francisco took seven to eight hours but was nonstop and therefore one unit. New York to Paris was nonstop and one air unit (ten hours, flying East). Johannesburg to Brazzaville was one air unit (six hours).

". . Suddenly, a clamor went up as at least fifty youngsters called out to join the fun. I ould toss the ball into a sea of waving arms and out it would come again."

Arrival at Tchibanga: A white man out of the sky can be a frightening experience.

28

With only one unit separating me from South Africa, the decision to make the additional stop was almost automatic. In this I had the encouragement of Alan Paton who, on his visit to New York some weeks earlier, said that even a brief visit would be well worth the journey. The trials of more than a hundred South Africans under the new, extreme "treason" laws were coming up in Johannesburg and this was a good time to see history in the making.

Clara, who had lived most of her life in Johannesburg, arranged an intensive schedule. I was to meet people who were intimately involved in the problems of the Union. This would include persons of varying political opinions and backgrounds—all the way from owners of large gold mines to African writers and nationalist leaders.

One of the persons Clara was especially eager to have me meet was Henry Nxumalo, one of Africa's leading journalists. His writings appeared regularly in *Drum,* a monthly magazine, and in *The Golden City Post,* a newspaper, of which he was news editor. *Drum* was written by Africans and claimed the largest circulation of any non-European magazine on the continent.

Several people referred to the fact that Nxumalo was presently writing a book on South Africa for an American publisher. His growing importance, I was told, was largely the result of his crusading articles. Everyone I met who knew him said he was one of the soundest and most courageous among African observers. His achievements in journalism were prominently described in the book *Drum* by its former editor, Anthony Sampson.*

Consequently, I looked forward to meeting him at dinner the first night of my visit in Johannesburg.

Nxumalo didn't come to dinner. He had been murdered earlier in the day.

Right then, I learned one of the main facts about life in the Union of South Africa. I learned that there are two worlds. One is the world of graciousness, spaciousness, and infinite natural beauty

* Published in London by Collins (1956) and in the United States by Houghton Mifflin (1957).

and color, heightened in its loveliness by crisp air and sparkling sun. Then there is the other world, made entirely by people. It is taut, harsh, violent. The charming villas by day become places to be closely guarded at night. When two men approach each other after dark, each is apprehensive about the color of the other. Thus, passing a person on the street at night takes on the aspects of an encounter. For when the sun goes down the coolness seems to enter the human soul and the mood of the land hardens.

I knew I could never begin to understand South Africa unless I could understand the nature of this change, unless I could comprehend the proximity of the loveliness to the terror, and the interrelationship between the two. Perhaps if I could find out about Henry Nxumalo—why he wrote as he did, why he was feared and why he was murdered—I might learn a little about the two worlds.

The newspaper obituaries established that Henry Nxumalo, thirty-nine, lived with his wife and five children in the "location" called Orlando, some miles outside Johannesburg. (Africans are not permitted to live in the city itself; they live in "locations"—most of which are slum areas consisting of old huts and shacks and some of which are new housing developments with their well-built though fairly small homes. Orlando was one of the earliest of such developments.)

Nxumalo was born in Port Shepstone, on the East Coast near Durban. He came from a Zulu family. Both his parents died while he was a boy. Henry's first job was as a kitchen boy in Durban. Like thousands of Africans, he found himself lured to the big city, Johannesburg; and he became part of a giant paradox. Once having left the way of life of the village or the small town, the Africans who come to Johannesburg seldom want to return. They resent the white man's world not because they are forced to stay but because they are not fully accepted. What they seek is not freedom to return to the village but freedom to live decently and honorably in the city.

Henry Nxumalo came to Johannesburg as a youth and worked in a boilermaker's shop. After hours he wrote poetry, which he sent to the magazine, *Bantu World,* and much of which was published. This led to a job as messenger for the *Bantu World,* of which he later became sports editor. He enlisted during the war and became a sergeant. This brought him to North Africa. At the end of the war he went to London. When he returned to Johannesburg, he resumed his writing for the *Bantu World.* In 1948 he married a nurse. In 1951 he joined the staff of a new magazine called *Drum.* The same publishing house also put out *The Golden City Post,* of which he became news editor.

His exploits on *Drum* and, to a lesser extent, in *The Golden City Post,* made him perhaps the best-known non-European journalist in South Africa.

Why was he murdered?

The facts of the killing were elusive. The body had been found on the dirt sidewalk of a crowded location. Heavy footmarks indicated a struggle. Several persons apparently had been involved. A trail of blood showed that Nxumalo had crawled more than fifty feet from the scene of the attack before he died. Robbery did not appear to be a motive for the killing; his valuables were untouched. The police had no theories.

Most of Nxumalo's friends were reluctant to talk; they looked away and said nothing. I spoke to a leader in the YMCA who had known Henry Nxumalo as a boy. He said that from the beginning of their acquaintance Henry had talked about wanting to be a journalist.

"He came to see me after he got the job on *Drum* and told me the kind of thing he wanted to do. He wanted to expose the brutal conditions of the jails. He wanted to write about forced labor on the farms. He was not a revolutionary. He believed that many white people who were in a position to effect basic reforms really knew very little about what was happening. And he had confidence in his ability to reach their consciences with documented facts."

I learned that after Nxumalo started his series of articles under the byline "Mr. Drum" he began to get threats of various sorts. But not until now had any of them materialized. At that, no one

". . Before I left, Mrs. Nxumalo handed me some photographs of her husband that had turned up while she was looking through his papers. They showed a young man with a strong, alert face. He was sitting at his typewriter."

Henry Nxumalo at home with his three children. The Nxumalo family had only recently moved to their house in the new Orlando "location" when this photograph was taken.

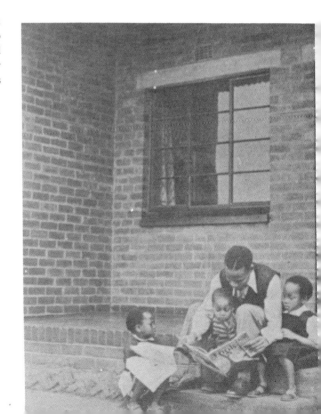

could say that any of these threatening letters had been received recently. Two close friends, however, mumbled their suspicion that it had been a political killing but would say nothing further.

I paid a visit to the publication offices of *Drum*. It was located just off one of the main streets in the heart of Johannesburg. *Drum's* reportorial staff was African, though the editor, Sylvester Stein, was white.

The arrangement of the office and the general atmosphere were more suggestive of a daily newspaper than that of a monthly magazine. I chatted with several men on the staff. They spoke freely about Nxumalo and his contempt for danger. They spoke, too, about his heartiness, his ready sense of humor, his joy of living.

"Despite everything that man went through, and it was quite a bit," said Zeke Mphahlele, himself one of the leading African writers, "Henry never became embittered. That's the most important thing for any writer, not to become embittered. Bitterness enters the eyes and keeps you from seeing the full story. It turns you away from the people you have to reach. All of us here envied Henry because he wasn't bitter. But we never knew how he managed it."

I met William Modisane, the music critic on the staff, who had been with Nxumalo only a short time before the murder. Mr. Modisane spoke about Nxumalo's part in building up the circulation of *Drum* until it became the biggest magazine by Africans for Africans on the continent. He told of the time Nxumalo committed a minor law violation in order to be put in jail, served his sentence, and then wrote about the actual conditions. There were official denials, but the reforms he called for came about.

Then there was the time that Nxumalo, disguised as a laborer, got a job on a farm in Bethal. He had heard that prisoners were being sent to Bethal in what amounted to forced labor. At Bethal Nxumalo was beaten up along with the prisoners. He worked alongside young men, not prisoners, who had been "recruited" on the understanding that they would be taken to an entirely different place but were shipped to Bethal and deprived of the right to leave.

The legal pretext for keeping them was that they had "held the pen." It is not necessary for Africans to sign their names to labor contracts. If they "hold the pen" over the contract, witnessed by a white man, the contract is considered to be binding.

The big need in South Africa is for human labor, and intensive efforts are made to recruit the Africans from the villages. Nxumalo was concerned both about the dishonesty of the recruiting and the dreadful conditions under which the men worked and from which there was no legal recourse. He escaped from Bethal, and presented the documentary evidence of what had happened. A large part of the continent was stunned by the disclosures and, once again, there were denials; but the basic reforms were made just the same.

Mr. Mphahlele and Mr. Modisane offered to take me to see various parts of Johannesburg that were indispensable for any understanding of the place. But first, I wanted to talk to *Drum's* editor, Sylvester Stein.

They brought me to Mr. Stein's office. Mr. Stein is a "European," as all white men, regardless of their geographical origin, are designated. I judged him to be about thirty-six. He was in the middle of a magazine deadline situation not unfamiliar to me. I watched sympathetically as he worked quickly to keep the production machinery moving. I could see that he knew his business.

Then, the copy cleared from his desk, Stein sat back and talked fully and openly. No, he didn't think the government had engineered the killing or was implicated in any way. Whatever *Drum's* political and social differences with the government—and they were substantial—he didn't feel that it would sanction murder as a technique for disposing of troublesome people.

"Things may be bad," he said, "but we're not dealing here exactly with a Hitler-type government. The Union is up to its neck in social injustices and problems, but it would be a serious mistake to confuse this government with the kind of dictator state that existed in Germany or Italy before the war or that exists under communism today. Exactly why Nxumalo was killed, I don't know. But you can be sure we're going to try to find out."

Stein went on to talk about Nxumalo's work for *Drum* and how, by exposing brutality and callousness, he had helped to effect important reforms. There was still some responsiveness to honest and dramatic fact-finding in the community at large. The executive and legislative branches of the government were responsible for the *apartheid* repressive legislation and restrictions. But a large part of the judiciary was still rigorously honest. And there was a considerable section of the white population which, even though it might go along with *apartheid* in general, balked about some of the specific aspects of *apartheid* in practice.

This was one of the many complexities that one came to recognize and respect in South Africa. Despite the iron will of the government about *apartheid,* the old forms of parliamentary government and judicial machinery were in large part preserved. This seemed at odds with the practices of the other branches of government, but you accepted it as part of the puzzle. Nor was the grand picture simplified by the sharp divisions among the whites—especially between the English and the Afrikanders (Dutch), with the latter now enjoying a preponderance in government. And even among the blacks, there were factions and frictions that not infrequently resulted in violence. This, too, was something that had to be taken into account before accepting or making any generalizations about the situation in South Africa.

Sylvester Stein's business was to deal with this complexity. It wasn't easy; the white world couldn't quite make up its mind about him because of his connection with the blacks. And the black world couldn't accept him all the way because he always had the privilege of retreating to the world which shut them out.

Stein's predecessor, Anthony Sampson, also white, had written about this predicament in his book.

"I could never explain [to whites]," he wrote, "that *Drum* was a job, and our readers were human like anyone else. I saw white people eyeing me as a crank; and I began to feel a crank. Probably I ostracized myself more than they ostracized me. In white society, I began to feel a slight chip on my shoulder.

"And as I penetrated farther into the world of the Africans, I found myself caught between the two camps of black and white. The contrast, from a cocktail party in the northern white suburbs to a drinking den in the southern black locations, was absurd . . .

"The contrast was stimulating. I saw one world in terms of the other, always slightly aloof: black against white and white against black."

Stein, like Sampson, had to cut across the barrier of *apartheid* constantly just in order to do his job. "At every turning are the signs '*Slegs vir Blankes* (For Whites Only),' '*Nie Blankes* (Non-Whites),' sorting the two races like an infallible machine, and sending them separate ways."

Once, Anthony Sampson and Henry Nxumalo stopped near a sign along the road reading "Natives Cross Here." Nxumalo turned to Sampson. "That sign is incomplete," he said. "It should read: 'Natives *Very* Cross Here.' "

Apartheid was more than a wall of color separation. It was a declaration of white ownership and control. It meant that the Africans, who constituted 90 per cent of the population, were limited to ownership of 15 per cent of the land. It meant that Johannesburg was out of bounds to blacks except for daytime working purposes. In order to commute to work from the locations, the Africans often had to spend four or five hours a day, much of it waiting for buses.

Apartheid meant a license just to live. An African needed a license to identify himself. He needed a license to work. He needed a license to be out of work. A passbook sometimes contained as many as six or seven separate items, each of which had to be countersigned regularly and kept up to date. Irregularities in pass-books—indeed, just leaving a passbook at home—could mean a prison sentence. It was in this way that Henry Nxumalo got him-self arrested in order that he could write about the wretched conditions at the local prisons.

"I could never forget about *apartheid*," Sampson wrote. "It cut across nearly everything I tried to do. It made the job of a white editor on a black paper awkward. I could never travel with Henry in the same train, taxi, bus, or lift. We could not be together in a restaurant, a bar, a theatre, or a park . . .

"Even in the contents of the magazine, *apartheid* intervened. We were ticked off for showing a picture of Eleanor Roosevelt shaking hands with Mrs. Edith Sampson, a Negro woman. We could not print photographs of a black boxer pummeling a white boxer. Mixed boxing is forbidden in South Africa, and photographs of mixed fights were frequently held up by the South Africans as constituting 'incitement.' "

Sampson had also written about the time that Nxumalo saw a white woman fall down in the street.

"I was just going up to help her," Nxumalo told Sampson, "and then I stopped and thought: what will the whites think? They'll think I'm trying to rape her. If I pick her up it means I'll actually have to touch her. A native touching a European woman! Oooh! Terrible! I couldn't risk it, so I walked on."

Ironically, it was the fearful reluctance of the Africans to become involved in difficult situations that may have cost Henry Nxumalo his life.

For his body lay on the sidewalk five hours before the police were summoned. It is possible that he bled to death during that time. Across the street was a hospital.

If Henry Nxumalo's own doubts about helping a fallen woman seem unjustified, it may be helpful to consider a statement made by Alan Paton, who for millions of white people around the world has served as their conscience in South Africa. Paton was speaking at a public meeting about both the ostracism and physical danger involved in direct contact with Africans under the existing strained circumstances.

"Who is there who would not hesitate to come to the aid of an African who stumbled in the street?" he asked. "And if you say that no one would hesitate, I must tell you that there is at least one, and he is speaking to you from this platform now."

In talking to Sylvester Stein, I learned that when he took over the editor's job from Sampson he was to go through the same personal difficulties and challenges—and also the same rewards. Things happened as the result of articles such as Nxumalo liked to write. And the magazine continued to grow. I had a strong respect for the problems involved in building a magazine; but I knew that such difficulties as I had experienced were minor alongside the challenges that faced Anthony Sampson and Sylvester Stein. And when the evidence came that the magazine was hitting its mark, the satisfaction was bound to be rich indeed.

"Yes," Sylvester Stein said, "I can't think of a more varied or exciting job than this. But every once in a while the ceiling falls in on you. That's the way I felt yesterday when I heard that Henry had been murdered."

I thanked Mr. Stein for his time, then rejoined Zeke Mphahlele and Bill Modisane. Zeke took the wheel of an old Chevrolet and we started on our tour. Our first stop was a narrow shopping lane which served as the supply headquarters for fetishers, or witch doctors. Store after store offered an endless variety of goods that are part of the witch doctor's trade—masks, ceremonial objects, magic devices, herbs, potions, processed foods.

"Just how important is the witch doctor in a place like Johannesburg?" I asked my escorts.

"Not as important as he used to be, but still a surprisingly large factor in the lives of the people," Zeke said. "Many non-Europeans still go to them when they are ill—and sometimes when they aren't ill."

The gap between the Africans who went to fetishers and those who didn't was a wide one, I was told. But the conflicting opinions held about fetishers were not the only major point of separation within the African community.

"An educated African has a hard time inside many of the locations," Bill said. "He is resented by his fellow Africans because of his knowledge and because he is believed to have an advantage over most of the other non-European people. The same would apply to any well-dressed African. And by well-dressed I mean any man who wears a tie. According to this standard, it is generally easy to pick out an educated African, for they are better dressed than the others. It is not unusual for educated Africans to be beaten up."

I asked whether it was possible that this was what had happened to Henry Nxumalo.

It was possible, they agreed, that it could have been something as simple as a random act of violence directed against a black man with a tie. But in Nxumalo's case, there were too many other factors to be taken into account. He took too many chances in the things he wrote about. Nor were his crusades limited to abuses by whites against blacks. Violence by black against black deeply concerned him.

"Henry was opposed to the gangs and everything about them," Zeke said. "He hated to see young boys drawn into these different gangs, each with its own names and dress and habits. One particularly strong gang is known as the Russians. There is no political significance to the name. They just happened to fasten onto the name; another is called the Berliners; and another the Americans, etc. The Russians like to walk around wearing brightly colored blankets. The Americans like to affect zoot suits.

"It makes no sense, but that is the way it is. And each gang makes its own laws. No one informs on crimes committed by fellow members of the gang—at least, not if he expects to stay healthy. Most of the gangs are tough, especially the Russians. They carry small arms, generally long switch knives."

The favorite reading of many gang members, I learned, was the American terror comics. And the favorite entertainment was the American gangster film. We were not without influence in that part of the world.

Then Nxumalo might have been a victim of one of the gangs, I asked.

Yes, it was possible; in fact, anything was possible, they said. But, once again, no one knew enough to be sure.

We were now passing through one of the locations where the "Russians" lived. I observed a group of ten or twelve young men wearing somewhat faded blankets in cape style. Zeke identified them and said it would be a good idea to stay away from this place after dark.

Soon we were in the famous black location or quarter known as Sophiatown. Many novels written about South Africa had their central settings here. Sophiatown was the largest of the locations. But it was now being closed down. Few reasons were given publicly. It was believed by some that the government felt Sophiatown was too close to Johannesburg, too likely to become the center from which mass violence against the whites might spring. Others believed that the government was genuinely concerned about the squalor and wanted to resettle the "natives" in the new housing developments that were now being built far outside the city.

In any event, the decision to condemn Sophiatown had been strongly resisted by the people who had to move. But the government was proceeding with its plan. Much of Sophiatown would be torn down, rebuilt, and opened up for settlement by whites.

Zeke discussed the situation in a matter-of-fact way. There was no bitterness in his voice.

I recalled what he had said earlier about Henry Nxumalo's ability to think and write without bitterness; and I told Zeke he had no reason to be envious, for it seemed to me that he had succeeded in that respect.

"I try," he said. "I try very hard. I am now writing a novel. Some chapters I have had to write over and over again, maybe as many as six times, because I am afraid that they sound as though they were written by a sour old man. There's so much around you that's hard to swallow that you've got to fight with yourself to get it down and keep it down."

We arrived at Bill Modisane's home. It fronted on a small courtyard. Some poorly dressed elderly people sat on the narrow stoop. They watched with faint amusement as a toddling infant tried to embrace a dog.

Bill invited me into his quarters. It was a single room made to serve all the purposes of a small family. Mrs. Modisane was not home at the moment. The room was about twelve by ten. It contained a large day bed, table, electric refrigerator, small stove, several chairs, and a bookcase. There wasn't much open wall space but it was adorned with several attractive modern paintings. What could have been a dingy cluttered thimble of a room had been neatly and imaginatively decorated.

As I mentioned earlier, Bill Modisane was a music critic. Noticing a small phonograph player, I asked Bill about his recordings. He said he didn't have much of a collection but he was hopeful that, circumstances permitting, he might be able to build it up and perhaps even obtain a high fidelity playing unit.

He served some refreshments. Africans by law are not permitted to possess or serve alcoholic drinks under penalty of arrest. On occasions the law is observed, more the result of economic limitations than determination to comply. The law, of course, does not apply to whites.

Bill discussed his hope that some day he might be able to bring his family to Canada or the United States. He was hopeful that he could get a job on a newspaper as reporter or music critic. He also wanted to study.

It was now late in the afternoon and I was due back in Johannesburg for dinner. We drove back under a deepening sky. The colors of the landscape responded to the warm orange of the western horizon. Man-made mountains of slag heaps from the gold mines, as characteristic of Johannesburg as skyscrapers are of New York, took on the color of gold itself. But the gold mines were also the center of many of the most deep-seated economic and racial problems of the country. Once again, I could reflect on the contrast of the beauty and the squalor, and the incestuous relationship that almost seemed to exist between the two.

When we came into Johannesburg, I saw long lines of Africans stretching almost endlessly. There was one large open area where the line wound in and out and around and was so long that I found it difficult to see the end of it. In some places the line would swell out until it was six or seven people thick.

The people were waiting for the buses to take them home. Sometimes they would have to wait two or three hours. The trip itself might take an hour. Allowing the same amount of time to get in to work early in the morning, Africans sometimes had to spend many hours or more each day coping with the ordeal of transport. And when the bus company announced an increase in the fares, it touched off a series of riots.

Africans are not agreed among themselves about the methods to be used in combating inadequate bus service or the fare increase. When a movement for a boycott against the bus lines developed in the Evaton location, thirty miles from Johannesburg, it was opposed by a large number of people. The boycott went into effect. On the next day, a clash took place involving about four thousand people armed with sticks and clubs. The boycotters were in the majority by a ratio of three to one. Two persons were killed. No one bothered to count the injured. Eight houses were wrecked. Not much attention was paid to it in the outside world, but a number of whites spent hours each day ferrying the Africans to and from their homes. The significance of these acts was not lost upon the black community.

Henry Nxumalo was especially concerned about the fact that it was illegal to engage in organized protest. The government had declared the protest activities were acts of communism which were outlawed under the Suppression of Communism Act.

I asked my escorts whether this didn't mean that anyone who tried to get people interested in working together to bring about essential reform—even though the problems involved were of a non-political nature—could be brought to trial as a Communist.

This was exactly it, they said. The government had charged one hundred and fifty-three people with treason under the Suppression of Communism Act. No one knew exactly what the charges were, but no one expected that the government would attempt to prove that the accused were *members* of the Communist party. If incitement to protest could be proved, then it was tantamount to communism, and communism was treason.

Johannesburg bus stop. "Africans sometimes had to spend many hours or more each
coping with the ordeal of transport. And when the bus company announced an increase
the fares, it touched off a series of riots."

"We drove out along the 'Main Reef,' as Johannesburg's principal artery is called. We pa
some of the largest gold mines and electric power stations, their mammoth vase-sha
water-pressure towers standing like giant sentries over the rolling countryside."

Some of the most distinguished Africans were now involved in the trials. Only a week earlier, preliminary hearings had been held. And now the entire nation held its breath, wondering what would happen next.

Once before, the government had been successful, through severe measures, in throttling a movement which challenged the ideas underlying *apartheid*. Manilal Gandhi in 1953 had attempted to organize a passive resistance movement along the lines made famous by his father in India. But the government used the jails and the lash with such resolute effect that the movement collapsed.

Bill Modisane and Zeke Mphahlele dropped me off at the private residence where I was staying in Johannesburg. I thanked them and told them of my desire to keep in touch with them. I knew that nothing would have pleased me more, on my return to the States, than to be able to help Bill Modisane to find a newspaper job in Canada or the United States, and to try to find a publisher for Zeke Mphahlele's new book.

That evening, after dinner, when we discussed the plans for the next day, I asked Clara whether it would be in order for me to pay my respects to Henry Nxumalo's widow. She said she was certain Mrs. Nxumalo would welcome my call. There were, however, some technicalities. Whites were not allowed to visit African locations without specific government authorization.

Clara said she would arrange with Dr. Ellen Hellman, a "European" and a distinguished anthropologist, to take me out to Orlando. Dr. Hellman, like Anthony Sampson and Sylvester Stein, moved in and out of both worlds in Johannesburg in the pursuit of her work and concerns. She had helped to organize and maintain joint councils for improving conditions between black and white. When prominent Africans got into trouble with the government for one reason or another, they could turn to her for advice. Her prestige and influence were considerable. She had helped to arrange bail for many of the accused in the treason trials.

Dr. Hellman picked me up in the morning. Our first stop was the old post office building where Dr. Hellman obtained the pass for the locations without difficulty. We then drove out along the "Main Reef" as Johannesburg's principal artery is called. We passed some of the largest gold mines and electric power stations, their mammoth water-pressure vase-shaped towers standing like giant sentries over the rolling countryside. The gold mines were having their troubles; prices had not kept pace with the inflationary spiral, and salaries were low.

The vast majority of the Africans who work in the gold mines are migrant laborers. They live in compounds furnished by the mines and usually patronize company stores. Food is furnished by the mine companies. The diet is well rounded and high in protein value, unlike the average diet of most Africans. The physical condition of the men who work in the mines is considered good.

Most of the migrant mine workers are signed up by recruiting agents for a minimum of a year. The big lure is city life and a chance to accumulate a modest amount of capital, something that is rare in village life.

At the time the young married males of the village "hold the pen" over the contracts to work in the mines, no doubt there is every intention to return to their wives and children at the end of their service. But it doesn't always work out that way. Some get caught up in city life or become involved in new domestic situations and never go back. The result is a permanent disruption in the home lives of thousands of families in the villages.

On the way out to Orlando we passed several of the older locations—vast sprawling collections of shacks and crowded alleys that lay on the land like a giant fungus. But we also passed new locations for Africans that were reminiscent of the Levittown type of housing development in the United States. The houses were small and repeated themselves endlessly, but they were neat, attractive, and sturdy. Rent was modest and convenient terms had been worked out for purchase by the tenants.

Some of these new developments near Johannesburg were spurred into being by the leadership of Sir Ernest Oppenheimer, the widely respected philanthropist and civic leader. Sir Ernest had made per-

Sundays, the mine workers who belonged to different tribes would put on their dances
fore large crowds of visitors. The musical instruments were almost exclusively percussion
d were home-made.

sonal contributions of millions of dollars to help get the housing projects started.

I asked Dr. Hellman whether we might stop and visit with some of the people who had just moved into a new house. She agreed; we stopped outside a home that couldn't have been completed more than a few weeks earlier. She went in first to explain the situation and find out if we would be welcome. I entered the home of a man who turned out to be a coal dealer. The rooms were small but pleasant. There was a good balance between window and wall space. There were four rooms, altogether, including the kitchen. I was impressed with the paintings in at least two of the rooms. The people couldn't have been more cordial or responsive.

We resumed our journey. At Orlando, we were delayed momentarily by the system of numbering houses not according to street but according to a general area. In any event, we found the Nxumalo home. Several people were standing outside. Three youngsters who turned out to be his children were sitting on the stoop. We introduced ourselves and learned that Mrs. Nxumalo had been called to the police station in connection with the killing. Henry Nxumalo's brother suggested that we wait. Then he said that everyone in the family was still completely mystified by what had happened. There had been some threats but Henry had convinced everyone that they were not to be taken seriously.

After about half an hour, Mrs. Nxumalo returned. She was a gracious, attractive young woman and she carried her grief with great dignity. After we were introduced she said the police had nothing new to report. They had asked her some routine questions which she had answered to the best of her ability.

I told Mrs. Nxumalo that I had heard that Henry had been writing a manuscript about South Africa for an American publisher. She replied that so far as she knew, the book was almost finished. She had the impression that her husband had asked someone a week or so earlier to read it, and she had no way of knowing whether the manuscript had been returned. In any event, she said she would be glad to look for it in the study.

Very methodically, starting with the top of a heavily cluttered table that had all the signs of being used for intensive research purposes, she began her search for the manuscript. While she was thus engaged, I glanced at some of the titles of books on the adjoining shelves—many of them having to do with literary criticism or collections of essays on writing. Among the authors represented were Somerset Maugham, Thomas Wolfe, Charles Morgan, Desmond MacCarthy, Cyril Connolly, John Dos Passos, John Steinbeck, Ruskin, and Proust. There were also a few books about writing for radio and television.

In the corner of the table was Henry Nxumalo's typewriter. In it was a sheet of copy paper on which he had started to write a story. In the upper right-hand corner were the identifying initials "nx"; in the center the slug line for the story—"pass"—and the number of the page. There were just a half-dozen lines before he broke off:

Last month a "Post" reporter was robbed of his pass in a Johannesburg township. He made a report to the police. But since then he has been arrested twice and paid a total of £2 in fines before he was issued with a duplicate pass. He got his new pass after weeks of going from one office to another—weeks of hardship, sweat, frayed tempers and wasted time, and it cost him 12/—.

When I read this I remembered something Bill Modisane had told me when he showed me his own passbook.

"If you want the story of hell, it's written right in this book. You see a policeman and instinctively you reach in your back pocket to make sure your passbook is there. When you're in a crowd you keep your hand pressed against it lest it be stolen. Sometimes, in the morning, you change your clothes and rush out of the house in too much of a hurry. Then after you arrive at your job you reach in your back pocket and you discover you left the book at home. And all day long you wonder whether you are going to make it, whether you are going to be able to get home that night. When you see a policeman you are so terrified you hardly know what to do.

"A curious thing, this dread we have of the police. I suppose in your country when you see a cop you feel reassured. In the U.S., if you are walking through a bad neighborhood at night and you see a policeman, a great deal of the fear goes out of the dark.

"But here the policeman is not the image of security and reassurance to us. If we are in trouble, the last thing we think of is the police. We look at a policeman and say, 'My God, I wonder if I'm going to be stopped. I wonder if I've got my passbook with me.'

"It's no fun being arrested and being put in jail for a passbook violation, not even under the reforms that have been put in as the result of the articles Henry wrote during his brief term in prison for being without his passbook."

It was ironic that the last thing Henry Nxumalo should have written was about the injustice of the passbook.

Mrs. Nxumalo interrupted my thoughts and said that the search for the manuscript was unavailing. She wasn't certain of the name of the American publisher but seemed to remember having received letters from Doubleday and Knopf asking whether her husband would be interested in writing about South Africa. She asked me if, when I returned to America, I might locate the publisher for whom Henry Nxumalo was writing his book and explain what had happened. She said she would continue her search and also attempt to find out if the book was still in the hands of a friend. It was arranged that when the manuscript was found she would mail it to me and I would undertake the necessary dealings with the publisher.

Before I left, Mrs. Nxumalo handed me some photographs of her husband that had turned up while she was looking through his papers for the book. They showed a young man with a strong, alert face. He was sitting at his typewriter. Another photograph showed him with three of his children in the doorway of his home

On the way back to Johannesburg, I asked Dr. Hellman about Mrs. Nxumalo's circumstances and who would take care of her.

"She's a registered nurse," Dr. Hellman said, "and no doubt she will be able to keep busy. But she has five children. I'm sure Henry's

ne of the photographs taken secretly for the magazine *Drum*, in the series written by Henry xumalo to expose prison injustices. "There was still some responsiveness to honest and amatic fact-finding in the community at large."

addition to the dog, several humans occupied this particular abode. The government was idertaking a resettlement program under which Africans would be moved into new housing ojects far outside Johannesburg proper.

friends, and there are many, will make up a purse for her or run some benefits. She has a lot of spunk. Even so, it won't be easy. It won't be easy at all."

Dr. Hellman was right about Henry Nxumalo's friends. Several days later more than one thousand people attended the funeral, and it lasted seven hours. All morning long at the Communal Mall people stood up to speak their tributes. Dr. Ray Phillips, one of his friends, said that if Henry Nxumalo's life and death were to have any meaning at all, it was that each individual had a fixed obligation to put an end to the terror that was disfiguring their society.

"Have we been shocked enough," he asked, "to grab the devil of hooliganism by the neck and say, 'This is as far as you go!'?"

The evening before we were to leave Johannesburg for Lambaréné, I checked notes with Clara Urquhart. I told her what had happened since I first began to find out about the questing, restless, wonderful Henry Nxumalo.

"No conclusions," I said, "just a lot of unassorted impressions. The Union is far more complicated than I had ever supposed."

"In that case, you're lucky to be leaving when you are," she said. "The longer you stay, the more complicated it gets."

"Sometimes it seems as though the trouble is actually a myth," I said. "Yesterday I sat on an attractive portico talking to reasonable people. I looked out over a rolling lawn toward a bed of tulips. Right then, all the turmoil and controversy seemed like a secondhand tale or a nightmare. Then I remembered the long lines of people waiting for the buses and I knew it was real enough. How long can it go on before it explodes?"

"The Africans are a remarkably patient people," Clara said.

"Even patient people have a sense of justice."

"Yes, but it's amazing how large the capacity of the Africans is to live with the impossible. And they're not easily stampeded into political movements of one sort or another. The Communists have tried hard to exploit the situation here but they've made hardly a dent."

"And yet the government feels sufficiently concerned about it to enact a Suppression of Communism Act," I said.

"Which has very little to do with communism. How many Communists are among the one hundred and fifty-three who are being accused of treason? If being aware of injustice makes a man a Communist, then we've just made Communists out of every great man who ever lived. The fact that the government uses the word doesn't change its real meaning."

I said I wondered whether the government's interpretation of protest as a Communist activity would stand up in court.

"That's the question almost everyone is talking about," she said. "I just have to believe that our courts have not lost their good sense or their independence. What other impressions have you had?"

I said I was struck by the fact that almost no one close to what was happening in the Union of South Africa had any clear answers. Everyone seemed to be groping. Another thing that impressed me was that the middle ground in South Africa seemed to be disappearing. Day by day, there was a growing accumulation of the forces at the extremes—the kind of extremes that made for mighty collisions and explosions.

"Most troubling of all," I added, "is the feeling I get that more and more people are losing interest in any moderate approach. I suppose there is nothing strange about this when we consider that the government itself has taken up its own position at one of those extremes."

"Isn't this another example of the hard time that moderates have had to face whenever the social problem becomes acute?" Clara asked.

"True," I replied, "but it bothers you just the same to see men and women of good will of both colors become increasingly lonesome in or near the center. Just in the process of existing, whether you are black or white, you find yourself being pushed toward the extremes.

"If you are black, you are confronted with the arguments of

those who have only to point to the policy of the government to prove that it intends to keep the African permanently disenfranchised—no citizenship, little personal dignity, even less land. According to this argument, the war has already been declared and it is only a matter of time before the fighting begins.

"If you are white, you are confronted with the arguments of those who say that whatever should or could have been done in the past, it is now too late to do anything except to hold fast For these whites, the issue seems to be simple: survival."

"One thing that makes the position of the South African whites so tragic," she said, "is that some of them have been here for centuries. This land and way of life they know and love. Where else can they go? What would they do? In the other parts of Africa, the white people have basic ties to the European countries from which they come or from which they may be only a generation or two away. And they feel they can always go back if they have to. Not so the white people of South Africa. This is their homeland. Their ancestors came here—many of them—about the time Columbus discovered America."

Yet the remarkable thing, I said, was that while almost every white person knew the explosion was coming, none was willing to say that it would come during his own lifetime. Thus a man of about sixty would say that matters could probably be kept in hand for another five or ten years. A man of fifty thought that the Union had about fifteen years of grace. A man of forty guessed that the big fireworks might not come perhaps for a generation. In the meanwhile, life goes on. And it is a gracious and congenial way of life, despite the occasional violence and subsurface tension.

"Even so, you have no idea," Clara said, "how much more tense it is than it was only a few years ago. That was when a middle ground seemed not only possible but inevitable. Now everything is so tight and uneasy. To be decent now requires martyrdom and I have insufficient courage."

She was talking very slowly, very deliberately.

"I've decided to give up my home in Johannesburg. I've been

fighting against that decision for perhaps three, four years. But how can I make my home here if I don't feel at home here? Everything is changing, and I can't make the changes in myself that have to go with it."

MUCH OF THIS conversation, and many of the things I learned when I tried to find out about Henry Nxumalo, came to mind during the flight over the jungle from Brazzaville to Lambaréné, when Clara said that the mood of Africa was changing and that there was a tightening in the air.

"In three or four minutes we ought to be able to see the Hospital from the plane," said Dr. Frank Catchpool from across the aisle in the Air France DC-3. "These pilots are very thoughtful fellows. When they know that some of their passengers are going to the Schweitzer Hospital, they generally make a run over the place."

Dr. Catchpool was right. We flew over the Ogowe River, which connects the South Atlantic with the interior of the middle Congo. From the air, the Ogowe was a light muddy brown. Here and there along the river, we could see small African villages. Then there was a cluster of buildings, with a church tower in the center. Dr. Catchpool identified this as the town of Lambaréné.

Then, suddenly, Dr. Catchpool called out and pointed to the Hospital. It consisted of a series of long, narrow buildings close to the river. Red roofs interrupted the jungle only briefly. Immediately beyond was the deep and endless green.

Approaching for a landing at the Hospital dock. Dr. Schweitzer calls out instructions to t
leper oarsmen in the pirogue. At the extreme right is the head of Dr. Frank Catchpool.

Same general scene, one minute later.

III

THE LAMBARÉNÉ AIRSTRIP, like all the others we had seen en route from Brazzaville, was just a dirt clearing in the jungle. The "terminal" was a large lean-to in which waiting passengers could shelter themselves from the sun. There were, of course, no mechanical installations or gasoline trucks for servicing the plane.

The reception committee at the airport consisted of Dr. Jan van Stolk and Mme. Oberman. Clara introduced us. Then, when they turned to Dr. Catchpool to inquire eagerly about his experience in the Brazzaville hospital for his dogbite, Clara told me that Dr. van Stolk was now the senior staff doctor at the Schweitzer Hospital. He was a native Hollander who had gone to medical school in the Union of South Africa and who had left a growing practice to come to Lambaréné. He was about thirty-two.

Mme. Oberman had worked with Dr. Schweitzer some months each year for about four years. She, too, came from Holland. (Many of the members of the staff, I later learned, came from Holland.) She worked in a general supervisory capacity, taking care of the needs of the Hospital personnel.

The entire party got into the back of a truck and sat on benches along the sides. I was thankful for the overhead canvas. It was noon and the equatorial sun was living up to its reputation.

"The path opened out on a courtyard, with low-lying wooden structures." Relatives hospital patients share in the daily work of servicing a community.

We drove for perhaps a mile and a half over a bumpy dirt road, alongside which were scattered African dwellings. Then we came to a clearing, just beyond which was the river. At the narrow wooden dock was a long pirogue, the sturdy and graceful native canoe specially built to withstand the powerful currents of the Ogowe.

Our bags were loaded into the pirogue by a half-dozen young men who comprised our crew. I sat up front near Mme. Oberman. Behind us were Dr. van Stolk and Clara and the young men who sang in rhythm to their strokes with the paddles. The trip to the Hospital is against the current, and so we stayed close to the shoreline. I marveled at the stamina, power, and good spirits of the young Africans as they paddled us upstream. And I recalled something that Dr. Schweitzer had written in one of his early books, *On the Edge of the Primeval Forest*. Shortly after he founded his Hospital in Lambaréné, it became necessary to take an emergency canoe journey into the interior. For hour after hour, the African natives insisted on staying at their paddles. It was an endurance feat that made a profound impression on the Doctor, and he resolved to remember it every time he was tempted to regard the Africans as shiftless or lacking in energy.

I recalled, too, that it was on his canoe trips that Dr. Schweitzer felt that conditions were most congenial for the exercise of the moral imagination. This I could readily understand. There is a total awareness of nature, if only because the contrasts are so compelling. The stillness over the water is made dramatic by the cries of the birds in the jungle. The sky is a silver sheath sparkling in the sun in contrast with the soft filtered light of the forest. The power of the current in the center of the stream contrasts with the easy play of the waters near the shore. I could understand why Dr. Schweitzer wrote that he could never take a canoe up or down the river without reflecting on the importance of reverence for life.

"The Doctor loves the river," Mme. Oberman said as if reading my thoughts. "Perhaps you will have a chance to take a ride with him in a canoe. When you do you will marvel at his expression, at his concentration."

I asked Mme. Oberman if the Doctor was in good health; some reports I had heard recently were disturbing.

"You will see for yourself," she said. "He is in fine health. His energy is high and he is in good spirits. Watch now; soon we will see the Hospital."

The Hospital is around a bend in the river and you do not have a good view of it until you swing around and come toward it downstream. In order to do this your canoe continues perhaps a third of a mile or more on the opposite shore beyond the Hospital so that when you cross the river the current will not carry you beyond the dock.

As the canoe swung into midstream, I discovered some figures dressed in white walking down the hill from the Hospital toward the small dock. Clara waved toward the shore. When we were about three hundred feet from the dock, I recognized the Doctor. He was at the edge of the dock now, waving to us. Then, when the canoe was within perhaps fifty feet, he began to call out directions. It was like a ferry being eased into her slip by commands from the bridge.

"À gauche! À gauche!" the Doctor cried out. "Lentement!"

Then, sharply,

"Arrêtez!"

He stooped and grabbed the prow, then eased the canoe alongside the dock. The Africans held the pirogue firm, and the Doctor reached over to help us out, one at a time. As he took my arm, he introduced himself, then went over to greet Clara warmly. He turned to Dr. Catchpool and inquired both about the health of the doctor and the health of the dog. Dr. Catchpool replied that he was well and that he had brought the dog back apparently none the worse for the experience.

The Doctor then took my arm and escorted me up the hill to the Hospital. The lane was narrow and we threaded our way past some small shacks and enclosures on the hillside. The ground underneath was moist and slippery and had the consistency of a chicken-yard. The reason was readily apparent. Almost everywhere I looked

Hospital Row and clinic. Arriving patients check in at the bungalow at the right.

Same place, late in the afternoon.

there were chickens, ducks, goats. Then the path opened out on a courtyard, with low-lying wooden structures. The building on the left was mounted on concrete piles about six or seven feet above the ground. This was where the doctor and the immediate members of his staff lived. Directly opposite were some utility and storage buildings, also set on concrete piles a few feet off the ground.

At the foot of the steps leading to the Doctor's quarters was Mrs. Schweitzer. I had been told she was not well and was able to get about the hospital grounds only with the greatest difficulty. The Doctor introduced me. Mrs. Schweitzer spoke in English; she was most gracious, apologizing for the fact that she was unable to accompany me to my room, and saying she hoped I would drop by for a chat after I got settled. We resumed our walk, the Doctor leading the way past several other frame buildings, each with its dark-red corrugated iron rooftop. One could hardly see the sky because of the thick benevolent overhead shelter from the trees. In a moment we were walking along the porch of a long single-story bungalow consisting of about twelve rooms for members of the staff.

The Doctor opened the door to my room, bid me rest a while, then come to the dining room for lunch. He apologized in French for the fact that he didn't speak English and said that the only place in the world where he would dare to speak English was Edinburgh, for the people there had a habit of speaking very slowly.

I thanked the Doctor and began to tell him how privileged I felt in being able to be with him at his Hospital. He cut me short with a wave of his hand, saying with a smile, *"Pas des compliments."*

The room was far nicer than I had expected. Walls and furniture were painted white. The room was only six or seven feet wide but it had everything one might need: small writing table and oil lamp, bookshelf, wooden cabinet for clothes, a stand for water basin, pitcher, and toilet articles. The bed was an iron four-poster, fairly narrow, with thin mattress. It was firm, just the way I like it, and did not sag.

One end of the room was screened in and opened out on the slope going down to the clinic and the Hospital wards. Beyond was the river Ogowe, shimmering in the midday sun. Some Africans in their pirogues were drifting downstream. It was warm, but not uncomfortably so. I was delighted with my first fifteen minutes in Lambaréné.

Clara came by to escort me to the dining room. There I met several members of the staff: Dr. Margaret van der Kreek, a lovely young lady of about thirty from the Netherlands, who was chief surgeon at the Hospital; Dr. Richard Friedmann, a Czech who had been imprisoned in German concentration camps during the war and who now performed the full range of medical duties required of a doctor at the Hospital; Mlle. Mathilde Kottmann, who had been the first to join Dr. and Mrs. Schweitzer at Lambaréné and who had served alternately as nurse, administrative assistant, housing supervisor, etc.; and Albertina van Beek Vollenhoven, a nurse in charge of one of the wards. Dr. Schweitzer explained that the rest of the staff was at work but that I would have a chance to meet them during the afternoon or at dinner.

I looked closely at the Doctor as he chatted with Clara across the luncheon table. His skin was pink and firm. His eyes were clear, his manner was alert. He was in excellent health. It seemed to me unbelievable that this vigorous, fully functioning man was about to mark his eighty-second birthday. When he had led me up the walk from the docks to my bungalow I had to step quickly to keep pace.

He asked about his various friends in the United States by name and I was happy to be able to tell him that they were all in good health. When he asked about Erica Anderson and Jerome Hill, who had just produced the motion picture about his life, I told him that I had seen a preview of the film and felt certain that it would be well received. I added that he was well on his way to becoming a movie idol in the United States.

He smiled. "Well, who knows, I may be famous yet."

One of the attendants came into the room with a baby gorilla

Dr. Schweitzer's bungalow in the central compound. The Doctor is chatting with a member of his staff at the steps of the porch.

C. U.

"The Doctor's eyes were clear, his manner was alert; he was in excellent health."

One of the non-working and perennially relaxed members of the Hospital community.

Dr. Richard Friedmann chats with "Joseph," who received his training as a medical attend at the Hospital.

clinging to her neck. She sat down on a bench in front of the wide window. The Doctor beamed every time he looked over at the gorilla. For the next few minutes he discussed gorillas and their high order of intelligence, saying that the gorilla was much closer to man in the scale of evolution than he was to the chimpanzee. Then he got up and walked over to the bench and took the baby gorilla in his lap. He put his head down so the gorilla could play with his massive head of unruly gray hair. Now and then the gorilla would tug fairly hard and the Doctor would wince, but say nothing. He had the look of an adoring grandfather.

As we left the dining room, the Doctor advised me to rest during the afternoon and to stay out of the sun.

The last thing in the world I wanted to do right then was rest. I went back to the bungalow, got my floppy rain hat to protect me against the sun, and then took off on an unescorted tour. I visited the central compound, where Dr. Schweitzer had his bungalow, and where the dining room was located. I walked down the slope to the clinic and the Hospital wards. Dr. Friedmann and Dr. Margaret were on duty at the clinic, handling the last few patients in the afternoon line.

Dr. Friedmann invited me to sit alongside him as he explained the kind of cases that turned up at a jungle clinic: venereal diseases, leprosy, malaria, hernias, framboesia, sleeping sickness, ulcerous sores, abscesses, malnutrition, miscarriages, toothaches. Not infrequently, patients would wait until their illnesses were advanced or their suffering acute before they came to the Hospital. Hence, the clinic more nearly approached an emergency ward than the outpatient department of a hospital.

An African of about fifty, his face betraying no pain, was next on line. As Dr. Friedmann examined the man, it was obvious he was suffering from a massive hernia. It seemed inconceivable that the man could get about.

"This is one of the astonishing things you come to accept as a matter of course in this part of the world," Dr. Friedmann said. "The people have an extraordinary fortitude. They don't usually give in to sickness unless it is so serious that it hobbles them. It is not at all unusual to find men like this, with hernias that would hospitalize white men at the very start, continuing at their work for many months or years before the weight and size of the sac make movement literally impossible. That accounts for the fact that so many of the hernias are strangulated. Much of the surgery done by Dr. Margaret here has to do with strangulated hernias. By this time she probably knows as much about strangulated hernia operations as any doctor in the world."

I looked over at Dr. Margaret—*"La Doctoresse"* as she was affectionately known to everyone at Lambaréné. She was busy filling out some prescriptions. I could readily understand why Clara had called her one of the most beautiful young women in the world. There was nothing mechanical about her appearance. Light-colored hair was combed straight back and held in place by a simple ribbon. She wore no lipstick or other make-up. Yet she possessed an unmistakable quality of classic loveliness both of feature and expression. I wondered about this attractive creature—how she happened to go into medicine and surgery, why she came to Lambaréné. Here was the raw material from which legends were fashioned.

A young African mother, her face heavy with apprehension, carried in a five- or six-year-old girl and set her down next to *La Doctoresse*. The child was wide-eyed and fearful. She clung to her mother's faded skirt with both hands.

La Doctoresse knelt down alongside the child and spoke to her reassuringly, then stroked her head as, speaking through an interpreter, she asked the mother the trouble. The mother said the child had persistent fever. Still kneeling and speaking softly, *La Doctoresse* took her stethoscope and applied it to the child's chest. Then, very deftly, she put a tongue depressor in the child's mouth. The little girl coughed involuntarily, then cried out. *La Doctoresse* reached behind her and took a little wooden doll from one of the drawers in her desk. She made small clucking sounds as she held the doll alluringly in front of the little girl. While the child scrutinized the doll, *La Doctoresse* lifted the child's dress and examined the lower part of her body.

Then she smoothed the little girl's dress and told her that it was all over and that she would soon be well again. The child smiled shyly, still holding the doll. *La Doctoresse* told the mother the child had malaria but that it could be brought under control. The child was assigned to a place in the wards and *La Doctoresse* wrote out instructions for her care and a prescription to be filled by the Hospital apothecary. Then she asked the African interpreter to have the woman repeat everything said to her, just to be sure she understood.

In keeping with the custom at the Hospital, the woman was asked whether she could afford to pay anything. Dr. Schweitzer believed that people are more respectful of advice, especially of a medical nature, if they have to pay for it.

The woman was prepared for the question. She opened her hand and offered *La Doctoresse* one hundred francs (equivalent of about twenty-five cents), an amount that was slightly above the average. *La Doctoresse* thanked her, then carefully made a notation of the revenue in the accounts book in which the daily fees from patients are entered.

I could see that the woman had something to say to *La Doctoresse* but was choked up. The heavy apprehension in her face was gone; now there was measureless relief and gratitude. I wondered what went through her mind as she looked at this white goddess with the golden hair who had such knowledge and skill as only the most gifted of men were supposed to possess. I could tell the woman was struggling for a correct way to make known her feelings. Then she reached out and lightly touched Dr. Margaret's arm. It was a simple gesture but profound in intent. Dr. Margaret responded with the smile not of a doctor but of one woman communicating with another in a universal language.

IT WAS TIME now to close the clinic for the afternoon. Dr. Margaret marked some notations in the accounts book, then closed her desk. We walked up the short hill to the bungalow where the staff lived.

"You must see my garden," Dr. Margaret said. "The jungle flowers are just now coming up."

In front of the porch leading to her room, Dr. Margaret had built a small wire enclosure of perhaps no more than six by eight feet. Inside, protected from the goats and other wandering animals, were the young shoots of jungle flowers. I couldn't identify them nor do I remember their names; but Dr. Margaret named them for me one by one as she ran a finger around the tender buds. What I do remember vividly is the joy and pride that this lovely girl doctor took in creating a tiny sanctuary for a few flowers.

It was late afternoon. The sun had lost its fever and a small wind came up from the river and eased the heaviness in the air.

Dr. Margaret sat down on one of the porch steps. It had been an exhausting day, and now she rested her head on her hands and breathed in the coolness.

"Do you like Lambaréné?" she asked. "It has all the things that are difficult to find outside. A chance to concentrate on your work; quiet when you need it; and most of all, freedom from all the non-essential things that fill one's life."

"Non-essentials?"

She looked at me sternly.

"Surely you must know," she said. "The non-essentials of life in Europe and America. The endless running around in circles to do things that seem a matter of life and death at the time but that you can't remember two days later. The business of struggling with a checking account at the end of the month to make sure there's enough to cover all the things that we bought but that we don't even know where to put. And the desperate way we try to entertain ourselves.

"Here at Lambaréné, we do nicely without the frills. We have a purpose and we apply ourselves to it. We never have to ask ourselves whether we are really needed. We are never at wits' ends for what to do with our time. When our work is over for the day we can sit down and rest or we can make our tea and we talk among ourselves or we can read and we can think. It is very good. Do you find this strange?"

I told Dr. Margaret that I had nothing but admiration for the people at Lambaréné and for their ability to come to terms with life.

"It may take you a little time to understand Lambaréné," she said. "So many people come here just for overnight and go away appalled. You know, there's a reason for everything at Lambaréné, but it takes a little time to find it out."

I said that I had been carefully indoctrinated by Clara and that I would do my best to get to know the real Lambaréné.

"That is good," she said. "Maybe you will not make the mistake of judging this as you would a modern hospital. It is a jungle village with a clinic. If Dr. Schweitzer had put up a fully equipped modern hospital of the kind you see in large cities, I am not sure the natives would come to it. They would probably be afraid of it. They must understand something before they give themselves to it. The hospital here they understand. It is very simple. If a person gets sick and the local remedies are of no use and the sickness stays on, the entire family gets into a pirogue and paddles—sometimes many, many miles—to the clinic here at Lambaréné. When they arrive, they find an African village very much like the one they left. If the patient has to be hospitalized, we assign the entire family to a cubicle in one of the shelters. The people go into the woods for their toilet and take care of their own refuse. They get their water from the wells. They cook their own food. They can get fish from the river. We give them bananas and some rice. They get the rest from the trees. We do the diagnosis and supply the medicines and check up on the progress of the patients. When they get better they go home."

"Do you manage to establish any real contact with your patients?" I asked. "Do you find yourself getting caught up in the lives of the people you treat so that you have a real emotional stake in what happens to them?"

Some babies are king-sized . . .

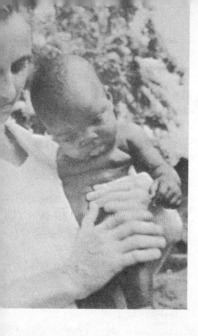

. . . while others fit comfortably into a hat.

c.

Three photographs of Dr. Margaret van der Kreek—*La Doctoresse*—chief surgeon at the Hospital. "She possessed an unmistakable quality of classic loveliness."

Dr. Margaret looked up. "It is true that there are many patients. So very many patients. Each day they come. It is hard to keep track of them. And many of them we see just once. But at the time they stand before you and tell you their story you make the contact. I think this has nothing to do with Lambaréné necessarily. It comes with being a doctor. A person comes to you and describes his ailment. You observe him carefully. You watch closely for a little sign that will tell you what you must know. And the patient will not have confidence in you if he senses that the contact has not been made."

I asked the question I had wanted to ask her since I first saw her in the dining room for the staff. I asked how it was she came to Lambaréné.

Dr. Margaret reached over the wire fence and ran her hand lightly along one of the young shoots. She said she had wanted to be a doctor ever since she was old enough to think about what she wanted to do with her life. Her father was an artist, her mother a poet. She grew up in an atmosphere of kindness, graciousness, and intelligence. She was aware that the great happiness enjoyed by her parents in their relationship to each other and her own resultant happiness were not the lot of all people. Her family suffered no deprivations, not even during the depression; and her father felt the obligation to do what he could to help others when he could.

All this created a determination in her to serve. Medicine seemed an effective way. Then she read about Dr. Schweitzer and his work in Africa. She doubted that the Doctor would accept her, but she decided she would get the most comprehensive medical and surgical training available and then volunteer. She knew that many of the persons on the Lambaréné staff came from Holland; at least she could get one of them to write a letter of introduction.

After she completed her internship the introductory letter was written to Dr. Schweitzer.

"Then very soon after that came his reply," she said, reliving the experience in her brightened expression. "He would take me. His letter was amazing. Dozens of details. He put each one down.

How I was to travel, what the timetable was, where I was to change trains and so forth, what my work would consist of in Lambaréné, how I was to go about making arrangements for passports, and the kind of clothes I would probably need. And there was an air of great kindness in everything he said.

"It is now two years since I arrived. At first, like most of the others who came, I was puzzled by many things, sometimes even disappointed. But the more I stay the more I understand and the stronger is my admiration for the Doctor. I know now why things are done the way they are.

"People know the Doctor as a great philosopher and theologian. I am lucky to know him as a human being. It is fantastic all the things he does every day and the things he manages to keep in mind. He has been after me for several months to take a holiday. I have been putting it off but finally I will leave. Next month I go to South Africa. A surgeon, Dr. Jack Penn, visited the Hospital here recently. There are new techniques in reconstructive surgery I want to learn. Dr. Penn invited me to work at his hospital. After I accepted, Dr. Schweitzer took it on himself to make all the arrangements for passport and visas. Only two days ago, he went in the pirogue to the village and filled out the forms. He brought back the forms for me to sign. Then, because there was some hurry in the matter, he took the pirogue again to the village and didn't return until long after dinner. Maybe he spent six or seven hours that day to save me the trouble. No detail escapes him. Everything has to be just so; and whenever he comes across something that he knows will be especially burdensome, he never asks someone else to do it, though we pray that he will, but goes ahead quietly and does it himself."

"Who will do your work while you are in South Africa?" I asked.

"Right now, we are very fortunate at the Hospital. We have enough doctors. You have met Dr. von Stolk. He comes from Holland, too. He is very young but he is very talented and he is very precise. Dr. Schweitzer leans on him heavily. Dr. Friedmann is a completely dedicated man. He has a fine background of experience. We have teamed up in the clinic and there is nothing about the operation of the clinic he does not know. You probably have heard that Dr. Friedmann lost all his relatives in the concentration camps of Germany during the war. He is not embittered. He asks only to be allowed to serve because he himself was spared. Then there is Dr. Cyril Coulon. He, too, is young. His wife is with him. Soon they will have a baby. They will have it here at the Hospital. Mrs. Coulon is such a fine young woman. The Coulons have worked in the jungle before. They are Dutch. They have gone out by themselves into the jungle villages to help supply medical help. Now they are here to help Dr. Schweitzer. Dr. Coulon knows the Africans well; he is a great asset to our staff. Dr. Catchpool you have already spoken to on the plane. He has not been here very long. He has done no medical work so far but I can tell that he has had excellent training. He is a sensitive man. There will be no shortage of doctors while I am gone. When I come back, Dr. van Stolk will go on leave for six months. There is always a great deal of rotation going on."

Dr. Friedmann came up the path and greeted us. He was soft spoken and there was shyness in his manner. He had an enormous jet-black mustache; it made me think of some of the photographs of Schweitzer at the age of thirty. When Dr. Friedmann sat down on the stoop and crossed his arms on his knees I could see, on the inside forearm, the number tattooed on him at the concentration camp. He would carry the number as long as he lived. He noticed that I was staring at it.

"Just a souvenir; you're welcome to look at it," he said, holding up his arm.

I told Dr. Friedmann that *La Doctoresse* had been telling me about her approaching holiday and about the things that led to her decision to come to Lambaréné.

"Actually, it is not much different from the rest of us," he said. "Some of us may have come here because we were in good circumstances and didn't feel quite right about it; others because they were in difficult circumstances yet managed somehow to survive, and they wanted to find some way of acknowledging their debt. But always it is the debt. And always you will find that somewhere we happened to read something by Albert Schweitzer that opened up a big door in our mind and made us know we had to come."

Just then, we heard explosions of joy from the far end of the porch. Three or four of the nurses were holding bright-colored dresses to themselves, their arms clasping the garments to their waists and their chins pressing against the necks of the dresses. They swirled around and squealed ecstatically.

"Dr. Margaret, come quick," one of them shouted. "Clara brought each of us a dress."

Clara was leaning against the porch railing near the end of the bungalow. Even at a distance I could see that she was deeply pleased.

Dr. Margaret jumped to her feet with the bright alertness of a child being offered a surprise gift. She ran down the porch. Clara reached into a box and took out a long blue cotton dress and handed it to Dr. Margaret who exclaimed her thanks and then rushed into her room to try it on. Three minutes later she emerged, smiling and radiant. The dress fit perfectly.

"Look at Margaret!" exclaimed Trudi Bochsler, the nurse in charge of the lepers. "She looks like a movie star. Only more beautiful."

Then the other girls rushed into their rooms to try on their own new dresses. When they returned, it almost seemed as though the place had been touched with magic. Each girl was proclaiming her delight with the appearance of the others. And indeed, each seemed uncommonly attractive. But more appealing than anything else were their expressions of satisfied wonder as they danced up and down the porch, their dresses swooshing and swirling.

"How does it feel to be Mrs. Santa Claus?" I asked Clara. She was beaming.

"You have no idea how much they hunger for the chance to dress up and do the attractive things most young girls take for granted," she said. "It's so easy to forget that even dedicated girls like this—girls of serious purpose and high intelligence—it's so easy to forget that they are still girls in every way—warm and wonderful and full of eagerness and feminine charm."

Albertina spun around and clapped her hands. "Tonight we will have a party," she exulted. "We will surprise Dr. Schweitzer. We will wear our dresses to dinner. And we will fix our hair."

Albertina was auburn haired. Even in the early evening light I could see that her face was flushed with excitement. Yet there was an essential quality of composure about Albertina that seemed to cause her to draw back as soon as she saw she had become the center of attention.

But Albertina never had the chance to develop any second thoughts about her suggestion, for the others seized upon it with whoops of agreement. They would wear their new dresses to dinner, they would put ribbons in their hair—and, some of them would use lipstick. They would all gather in the dining room several minutes early and would be in their places when the doctor walked in.

The plan was a complete success. When Dr. Schweitzer walked into the dining room, the girls—scrubbed, shining, bright-eyed— were all wearing their new dresses. They were sitting in their customary places, trying to make it appear that nothing special had happened.

The Doctor, in a split second, took it all in. His eyes danced behind the craglike brows. I could see he had a vast delight.

"Thank you for letting me come to your banquet," he said in the manner of a man who had just arrived at the Queen's ball. Then, when he sat down and the customary silence occurred so that he could say grace, he said that he was so overwhelmed by all the beauty around him that he had forgotten all the grace prayers he ever knew.

The girls were charmed and showed it. Then the Doctor leaned forward in the manner he adopts when saying grace, and the entire table became silent. I couldn't help noticing that the prayer of thankfulness had a special meaning for everyone on the staff.

Dinnertime at Lambaréné.

The Doctor finished saying grace and looked up.

"I, too, have a contribution to make to the festive banquet," he announced. "A case of wine that was sent here some time ago and has been waiting for just such an occasion as this. It is a very fine burgundy. We will all dine superbly tonight and drink to each other's health. And tonight—there will be butter!"

The mood of the staff that evening, like the wine itself, had a delicious sparkle to it. Only a few hours earlier, nothing out of the ordinary had been anticipated. Then, suddenly, the evening had been transformed into a surprise party—and each person was the guest of honor.

I looked around the long table. The men were obviously pleased with the sudden assertion of femininity by Dr. Margaret and the nurses. Three of the four male doctors were young and unmarried. While the men were certainly not unaware of the attractiveness of the young women on the staff at any time, their appreciation under ordinary circumstances was subordinated to the unending demands of the Hospital. For the main part, their relationship was professional. But now, for the moment at least, the circumstances had changed. The dining room was transformed into a small banquet hall and young ladies, gay and lovely, adorned the table.

It was interesting to see the way the occasion affected the conversation. Usually the people on the staff spoke about the work of the day or about matters related to the Hospital. But now, appealing nonsense was in order.

"Dr. Schweitzer, we want you to settle a bet," Dr. Margaret said. "Trudi and I have just been talking about champagne and how it is made. She says it is made just like wine and I said it can't be because of the fizz and the sparkle in it."

Dr. Schweitzer was equal to the occasion. For almost five minutes he expounded on champagne—how it was developed historically, what goes into it, why it is expensive, what kind of water is necessary, how it is bottled in order to keep the carbonation, etc. It was an astounding *tour de force* on the one subject in the world that he might be expected to know least about.

Neither Dr. Margaret nor Trudi had been completely correct and the bet was declared a stand-off.

Then the conversation somehow veered off into playwriting and acting, and from there into exploration and geology, and finally into furniture-making. On each subject the Doctor would listen carefully and then come forward with a surprising wealth of observation backed with historical information, dates, and intricate detail. With respect to furniture, the Doctor identified the soft woods and the hard woods, spoke vividly of their uses, the relative expense in their manufacture, and the competitive problems in the world market for fine woods.

Whenever the conversation seemed on the verge of getting too heavy, the Doctor restored the mood of gaiety with an amusing anecdote, which invariably had a point to make. One of these anecdotes grew out of a question on the declining powers of observation of older people.

"Naturally, it all depends on the person you are talking about," he said with mock seriousness. "When I was a boy of sixteen, I was very much under my grandfather's thumb. One day a cousin of my age of whom I was very fond came to visit me. We wanted to leave the house for a certain purpose but feared Grandfather might not give us permission. And so we told him we wanted to visit our uncle some blocks distant, and he said we might go.

"When we were out of viewing range from the house, we turned sharply and went in the direction of our real destination—a beer tavern. After we were there about ten minutes a man sat down at our table. It was our grandfather.

" 'An old man isn't as blind as you might think,' my grandfather said. 'And sometimes he is just as thirsty as younger men. Why didn't you invite me to come with you in the first place? Now pour me a drink.' "

Then Dr. Schweitzer looked at me with a twinkle in his eye.

"I'd better be careful," he said, "or Mr. Cousins will think I do nothing except tell funny stories."

The meal came to an end. The Doctor reached up and took his

napkin out from his open collar, folded it carefully, and put it in his holder. The hymnbooks were passed out and the Doctor announced the number of the hymn to be sung that night.

It was then that I experienced the shock of watching him sit down to play the dilapidated old upright piano. But all the others were long accustomed to both the sight and sound, and it did not diminish the general festive air of the party. And so tonight they sang with added spirit, still flushed with the brightness of the occasion. The Doctor finished the hymn, returned to his place and read the Lord's Prayer in German. Then, the dinner over, the staff went to the small side tables, carrying an extra cup of coffee and tea, so the mood would not be broken, and they would chat and relax in the cool of the evening.

The Doctor said good night and went back to his room to submit himself to the inevitable tyranny of his correspondence.

I walked back to my room, turned on the oil lamp, and wrote home to Ellen and the little girls. I was anxious for them to know about a place called Lambaréné and the people who worked there. For nothing is more essential to young people than to have their natural idealism nourished—and this I felt I could give them through what I had seen in my first day at Lambaréné.

Long after I turned off the small light from the kerosene lamp, I lay in bed listening to the sounds from the open wards a short distance away. There was a hacking cough, and then a child's cry. They were contrasting sounds to the ones I had heard a short time earlier in the dining room, but it was part of the human mixture and it was real.

IV

THE NEXT MORNING, I rose early in order to see the Hospital starting up on a new day. African women, wearing their blankets or faded colored cloth in wrap-around style, were carrying water jars on their heads and were on their way to and from the wells. Some of them had babies riding on their hips in a sort of side-saddle arrangement. In front of many of the rooms or cubicles in the open wards, women were cooking over homemade burners. I noticed one woman squatting close to an improvised stove consisting of a large pit in which she was making a banana milk stew for her family. The milk was her own. She deftly worked each breast close to the pan, sending streams of her milk into the stew. Here was the eternal woman in the oldest drama in the world—giving her totality to the cause of life near her, infinitely resourceful, inventive, responsible. The banana milk stew sent up its steam and the woman sang softly.

I continued down the path past the long rows of open rooms. African women were helping to wash the ill members of their families. A father of about thirty was playing with his little girl, throwing her into the air and catching her just above the ground. My homesickness was too much; in no time at all I managed to join the party and both of us entertained the youngster.

One of the main occupations at the Hospital is ministering to new life.

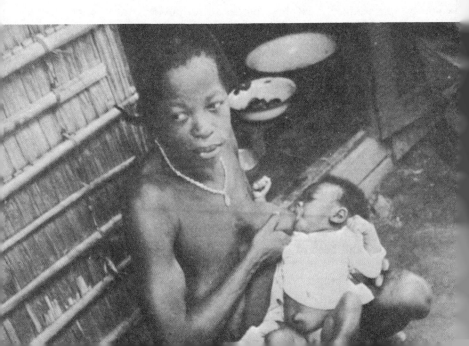

C.U.

...e of them had babies
...g on their hips in a sort
...le-saddle arrangement."

To my great relief, I was still able to perform the trick I used to play on my own youngsters—reaching behind their ears and finding all sorts of strange objects—pennies, pencils, rubber bands, and buttons. Then the three of us walked down to the dock, the child riding between us on our outstretched arms as we skimmed her over the ground.

The African father's name was George Malthen. I spoke to him in French and learned that his wife had just suffered a miscarriage. He had brought her and their child to the hospital just one day earlier. There were no complications, and she was now resting comfortably. Dr. Margaret had told him that in another two or three days she would be well enough to go home.

I asked where home was. He said it was up the river perhaps eight miles from the Hospital, where he worked at a lumber camp. He had had enough schooling to learn to read and write French, but that was all. He lived with his wife and child in a compound built by his wife's grandfather who was still alive.

Two years earlier his wife's sister had died during childbirth. The baby had been thought to be overdue and the local midwife tried to induce labor. Then, when the woman's condition became serious, the witch doctor or fetisher was brought in. The woman was given potions and made to do strange things. Then external force was used on her abdomen. The woman went into labor and died.

George Malthen said he resolved then that he would never let anything like this happen to his own wife. And when, several days ago, his wife began to bleed, her mother summoned the fetisher who told his wife to do strange things if she wanted to save her baby. When George said he wanted his wife to go to the Schweitzer Hospital, the fetisher warned him not to interfere or he would cause him to turn into a vampire at night and kill his own child.

"He told me he would cause me to kill again and again and then I would be killed myself."

"Were you frightened?"

"Yes, I had much fear. The fetisher, he is a powerful one. But I could think only about my wife and what had happened to her sister. And very early in the morning, before the sun came up, I carried my wife and child down to the dock, put them in my brother's pirogue, and paddled as fast as I could to the Hospital. I am glad, very glad, I have done so."

"And what will happen when you return to your village?"

George Malthen said nothing for a moment or two. His eyes were fixed on a pirogue not far away.

"I have not thought much about that yet. I don't know what the fetisher will try to do to me. I will try to be strong. I have seen people under the spell of the fetisher do terrible things. Other people who have disobeyed him have lost their minds or have died. It is a strange power he has. I must be strong."

As he spoke, I thought back on something Clara had told me about the witch doctors at Lambaréné. They would hover on the perimeter of the Hospital, weaving their spell on the patients or members of their families as they came within range. Generally, the witch doctors wore Western clothes, complete with white shirt and tie, though the outfit would be somewhat frayed and unpressed. Occasionally, they would affect the long diplomat's frock, wing collar, and black tie—again of a distinctly secondhand origin. They would warn the patients to leave the Hospital and place themselves in the fetisher's hands. The usual threat has to do with visions of human beings transformed into vampires in the middle of the night and sucking the blood of loved ones, sometimes until death.

Once, the entire leper village was tied up when a witch doctor of obvious persuasive ability caused virtually the entire African population to refuse any treatment. Patients went on a no-treatment system. Dr. Schweitzer was angry and he was all for finding the fetisher and settling the matter once and for all.

Even before the Doctor got to him, however, Clara had managed to persuade the fetisher to call off the strike. Clara is about five feet tall and looks as though she barely weighs one hundred pounds. I had an image in my mind of this lovely, dainty little lady confronting the African witch doctor in his stained diplomat's frock, trying to convince him to rescind his authority and abdicate. Later,

Clara refused to tell exactly what transpired at the meeting or what superior magic she herself had brewed in order to persuade the African to cease and desist. Whatever it was, it worked, and the patients submitted to treatment and diligently took their medicines.

When I asked Clara at least to tell me how she felt during her parley with the witch doctor, she knitted her brows:

"I was terrified," she said, "that what the Africans said about him might be true. I expected at any moment that he might get a big hex out of his black bag and turn me into a vampire right on the spot."

She shivered, then smiled: "Now let's not talk about it any more."

The rational-minded Westerner finds it easy to scoff at the hold of the fetisher over many Africans. But before we give ourselves too much credit, we ought to take into account the countless millions spent each year in America and Europe on mediums, bogus doctors, tea-leaf readers, numerologists, astrologists, to say nothing of snake oil, cure-all drugs, and quack potions for revitalizing the blood. Both the quacks and the witch doctors can point to people they have treated who have become well again. The human body has an amazing capacity for overcoming both natural illness and mistreatment by those who profess to cure. Indeed, even in the West, doctors today are amazed that people should have been able to undergo without too much apparent harm the kind of medical treatment that not so long ago was considered routine. We need also to remind ourselves that George Washington's physician tried to treat his patient for a cold by bleeding him. It may or may not be a coincidence that Washington died shortly thereafter.

In any event, the witch doctor has had—and still has—vast power in many parts of Africa. And his exploits are sufficiently dramatic for him to maintain the myth of his magic. While standing on the dock talking to George Malthen about his own experience, I recalled an incident that had been told me by Laurens van der Post of the Union of South Africa, one of the most sensitive and skilled writers to deal with the terrifying complex subject of Africa. His *The Dark Eye in Africa* is a poetic and rich presentation of the human situation in contemporary Africa.

Colonel van der Post had been in New York several weeks before my departure for Lambaréné, and discussed some of his own experiences with witch doctors in the southern part of Africa. He liked to visit African villages in the remote interior. Knowing the ways of the tribes, he would wait with his African guide and companion just outside each village until, eventually, one of the elders would come out to look him over, and, if he were lucky, to bid him enter.

On this particular occasion, van der Post and his guide had to wait several hours. Finally, they were confronted by the witch doctor, who was apparently torn between the natural curiosity and friendliness of the villagers, which led them to want van der Post to come in, and his own need for a sense of superiority, which led him to try to keep van der Post out.

The witch doctor casually said he would permit van der Post and his guide to enter on condition that they would agree to a test of comparative magic which the fetisher would name.

Van der Post readily accepted.

"The fetisher smiled in triumph," van der Post told me, "then bid me follow him. Inside the village a large crowd quickly surrounded us. The fetisher announced that the white man had accepted his challenge. Then the fetisher handed me his staff; it was about four feet long. He told me to instruct my African guide to keep the staff planted on the ground.

"This was to be a test of power. The fetisher said he would cause the staff to rise despite anything my African guide could do to keep it on the ground. My job was to exert all the influence I could on my African guide to keep the staff from rising.

"I had known Joseph, my African companion, for a long time. He was with me all the way. He understood exactly what he was to do. He stripped to the waist, revealing a gleaming and powerful torso. Then he took the staff and plunged it into the earth as far as it would go. He spread his legs apart to assure his balance, grasped the top of the staff with both hands, and anchored it firmly to the ground.

"I announced we were ready for the challenge.

"The witch doctor seemed unimpressed with the sight of my companion leaning on the staff with his full two hundred pounds. Then the witch doctor began his magic incantations. He made large swirling motions with his arms above the straining, sweating body of my guide, clinging to the staff.

"Then the witch doctor, in African, began to chant: 'Let the staff rise! Let the staff rise!' Some of the villagers had their drums with them and took up the beat. Within a minute or two, hundreds of people joined the chant. The drums beat louder.

"I watched my companion. Joseph was sweating profusely. His eyes seemed somewhat glazed and they were fixed on the witch doctor who continued his swooshing and swooping motions. And all the time the witch doctor kept chanting, 'Let the staff rise! Let the staff rise!'

"I began to feel uncomfortably warm. My shirt suddenly seemed to have the weight of a winter overcoat. And all the time the drums got louder and louder, merging with the chanting of the crowd. The volume of the sound was unbelievable.

"Joseph kept the staff pinned to the ground. I thrust my wet face next to his and shouted to him above his din to hold on. His muscles were taut and knotted with strain. His eyes were bulging in their sockets. The staff seemed secure under his weight.

"The chant approached its crescendo. Its beat was irresistible. Strange words began to form in my throat and on my lips. Almost before I realized it, I found myself intoning hoarsely with the others, first in a husky whisper, then in full voice: 'Let the staff rise! Let the staff rise!'

"The cords were standing out on Joseph's neck and shoulders. His arms and hands were quivering. There was a moment of agony on his face, then the staff began to waver in his hands. The witch doctor swooped even closer. The staff in Joseph's hands began to rise.

"He held on to it with all the remaining strength he could muster, but it was no use. The staff rose perhaps eight inches above the ground, Joseph clinging to it all the way. Then the witch doctor clapped his hands. The drums stopped, and the spell was broken. Joseph relinquished his grip and the staff fell to the ground.

"The people began to disperse. There was neither elation nor triumph in their manner. What had happened had been entirely expected and predictable. The only excitement would have been if the witch doctor had failed.

"As for the witch doctor himself, he couldn't have been more friendly. Now that he had demonstrated the inferiority of the white man, there was nothing more to prove; and he bid me welcome. We couldn't have enjoyed greater hospitality at that village that night if we had owned it.

"The next day, several hours after we had left the village, I decided to speak my mind to my African guide and companion.

" 'Joseph,' I said, picking my words carefully, 'how did you ever let yourself fall for that old hypnotism trick? That staff rose from the ground only because you lifted it. You were hoodwinked by one of the oldest witch doctor tricks in Africa.'

" 'Colonel,' he replied, 'I'll be glad to tell you why I couldn't hold that stick to the ground if you tell me why you kept screaming in my ear to let it rise.' "

WALKING AROUND the Hospital with George Malthen as my guide, I could understand why some visitors came away with negative impressions.

The idea of a hospital creates instant images in the mind of immaculate corridors, white sheets, total sanitation. These images were badly jolted when one saw the Hospital at Lambaréné for the first time. Countless numbers of goats wandered at will all over the place; even when they were not visible their presence was perceptible. The ground was made moist and slippery by an equally large number of chickens. Hanging heavily in the dank air was the smoke from the dozens of crude burners used by the Africans for their cooking. There was also an inexplicably sweet and somewhat sticky smell—perhaps from the cooking or from fallen and fermented fruit.

The sanitary facilities were at an absolute minimum. There were only two outhouses, one for each sex. The sewer underneath was open and sometimes the wind blew from the wrong direction.

There were no bedsheets. The Africans brought their own blankets. There were no "wards" as the term is used elsewhere. There were long, bungalowlike affairs with small cubicles. When a patient came to the Hospital, he was generally accompanied by his entire family. The mother did the cooking, as she would at home. The children were usually on their own.

The difficulty, of course, was with the term "hospital" as applied to the Schweitzer colony. It created false images and expectations by outsiders. The proper term should be "jungle clinic," as Dr. Margaret had explained. Dr. Schweitzer did not come to Africa for the purpose of building a towering medical center. He came in order to meet the Africans on their own terms. What he built was an African village attached to a functional medical and surgical clinic. The Africans were attracted to Schweitzer because of the man himself and because this was a village and a way of life familiar to them rather than a forbidding building where they would be cut off from their families and frightened by a world of total whiteness, of people and walls and machines. Modern medicine has come to accept the emotional security of the patient as a vital part of any therapy. Dr. Schweitzer knew this almost a half-century earlier when he made his plans to serve in Africa.

Most visitors who stayed long enough became aware of these things. While they might never be able to accept completely all the crudeness, at least they developed a working perspective. Some visitors, however, could hardly wait to get back to Europe or America in order to make known their discoveries. I had read at least four articles by disillusioned visitors to Lambaréné who misunderstood and misjudged Dr. Schweitzer and what he was trying to do in Africa.

In addition to exposing the lack of sanitation, the articles would invariably talk about the gruffness of Dr. Schweitzer, especially toward the Africans. They would be disturbed especially by his references to the "noble savage." These were some of the things that Clara Urquhart had cautioned me about before I left for Lambaréné. I, too, was surprised when I first noticed it, but after a while I realized it was more apparent than real.

The Doctor would bark out his orders to the Africans and scold them when they were doing something wrong. The impression he gave was that he was dealing with children. There did not seem to be sufficient respect in his manner toward the Africans. But this was not the complete story. To get the full picture, one must realize that Schweitzer also treated most whites as his "small brothers" and one had to find out how the Africans themselves interpreted his manner.

I watched the Africans closely as they worked under Dr. Schweitzer's orders, pushing back the jungle or gathering up stray pieces of lumber or moving crates of medicines. When he appeared to be arbitrary or gruff in what he told them to do they would smile broadly and carry out his instructions. Sometimes when he called out sharply, he would have a glint in his eye which they would catch and it would amuse them.

In talking to one of the African leper workers at some length, I learned that the ones who had been with the Doctor for any length of time had no trouble in understanding him. They knew he was somewhat short-tempered when things did not go just right; but they knew something, too, about the pressures under which he worked. And what was most important to them was that they knew the stern manner did not reflect any displeasure by Dr. Schweitzer.

Even when the Doctor seemed to lose his temper, it was only for the moment, the leper said. Sometimes, if he had been too severe, he would go out of his way later to make amends. Once he scolded the wife of one of the patients. Fifteen minutes later he beckoned to her when no one was looking, said he was sorry and gave her thirty francs.

"We do not become angry," the leper said. "How could we? Could a man become angry at his own father for telling him what to do?"

The fact that Dr. Schweitzer's role at Lambaréné was that of father—with respect to patients, their families, the workers, the white doctors and nurses, and even the visitors—is vital to any understanding of his manner. He had a sense of total personal responsibility for everyone and everything at Lambaréné. Time was his most precious commodity and he was no longer able to expend it in lengthy and cordial explanations for what he would like to see done. When, for example, he ordered the staff and visitors to wear pith helmets, he did not have time to explain that when he first came to Lambaréné he had to deal with serious cases of sunstroke suffered by white people who had insufficient respect for the striking power of the equatorial sun. Once he had to take an overnight trip by canoe to attend the wife of a French planter who became seriously ill because she thought it was unnecessary to wear a helmet even though the sky was overcast. She hadn't understood that even the diffused rays of a hidden sun can cause trouble. Dr. Schweitzer did not intend to use all his time in Africa treating white people for sunstroke; his purpose was to provide medical treatment for Africans. And it became a little wearisome having to go through detailed explanations to each new visitor. Hence his "take-my-word-for-it" approach, whether with respect to sun helmets or other matters, each of which had its reasons.

At Lambaréné I realized that the criticism of Dr. Schweitzer's relationship with the Africans missed an important point. The somewhat arbitrary or patriarchal manner was not reserved for blacks only. Once, while Dr. Schweitzer was superintending a jungle-clearing operation, he ordered the blacks to rest. Then he turned to three white members of the staff and to me and said, "Now it's your turn." We obediently took up the work, pulling stubborn weeds from near the trunks of young trees. After about ten minutes we looked as though we had been working ten hours. Our white shirts and khaki pants were drenched. All the while the Africans stood by, looking on us with boundless compassion and appearing desperately eager to spare us further effort. Then the Doctor said we could stop; he just wanted us to have some respect for the requirements of physical labor in Lambaréné. He had made his point.

Not infrequently, his seeming brusqueness was leavened with humor. When Adlai Stevenson visited Lambaréné he was escorted on a tour around the Hospital by the Doctor. The former presidential candidate noticed a large mosquito alighting on Dr. Schweitzer's arm and promptly swatted it.

"You shouldn't have done that," the Doctor said sharply. "That was my mosquito. Besides, it wasn't necessary to call out the Sixth Fleet to deal with him."

Clara gave me another illustration of the fact that his sternness knew no color lines. Once, he became particularly exasperated at an African who was putting boards of lumber in the wrong place. He mumbled that he could almost slap the man. Clara, who was standing nearby, was shocked and said so to the Doctor.

"Well, Clara," he said, "I don't think I am going to slap him. But if I should do so, I want you to close your eyes and imagine that I am slapping a white man. In that case, it will probably be all right with you."

V

BY SEVEN A.M., the sun had claimed the sky and the moisture was heavy in the air. I was halfway down the path leading to the dining room when Dr. Catchpool fell in alongside me.

"Better not let Dr. Schweitzer catch you without a helmet," he said. "He's very sensitive on this subject. He's had some experience with other people who saw no reason for wearing a helmet when they were going to be outside for only a few minutes. He's had to hospitalize them, and if there's one thing that annoys the Doctor, it's taking care of people who have no right to be sick."

In the dining room at breakfast, a few minutes later, Dr. Schweitzer referred to the matter. He instructed Clara to be sure to get a helmet to fit me from one of the extras in Mme. Oberman's possession. Clara nodded knowingly, then whispered to me that the Doctor meant business.

Breakfast consisted of thick homemade bread, jam, warm milk, coffee, and bananas. The Doctor ate somewhat more heartily than the rest. He supplemented the regular fare with an avocado pear and an egg.

Toward the end of the meal, I told Clara that I hoped we might have a chance to spend a few minutes with the Doctor. I didn't want to impose on his time, but I did have a few commissions that I felt ought to be performed as soon after my arrival as possible. During the course of a correspondence with President Eisenhower on various subjects related to the peace, I had mentioned that I hoped to be able to visit Dr. Schweitzer in Lambaréné at about the time of his eighty-second birthday. The President proceeded to write a letter of birthday greetings to Dr. Schweitzer which he was good enough to ask me to deliver. In that letter he spoke of his high admiration for the Doctor, saying that he had derived much inspiration from his work and thought, and felt the world was greatly in need of the kind of contribution he had been making. He ended by wishing the Doctor many more years of effective service to the human community. I had another message for the Doctor from Prime Minister Jawaharlal Nehru, whom I had seen on his visit to the United States in the fall of 1956 and who was most eager to have conveyed to the Doctor his deep admiration and affection.

I had a third commission. A fifteen-year-old boy by the name of Marc Chalufour in Concord, New Hampshire, was engaged in a crusade to save an old organ in his church from being replaced with an electronic instrument. He felt the old organ could be repaired and that it was sacrilegious to let it die—especially since he did not feel the new machine was really an organ. When, through one of his teachers, who was a friend of mine, he happened to learn of my coming visit to Lambaréné, he asked if I might deliver a letter from him to the Doctor. He felt that if he could enlist the Doctor in his crusade, he might win his fight.

I knew I would feel better when these various commissions were out of the way. And so I asked Clara what she thought would be a convenient time to act. When the Doctor got up from the break-fast table, Clara followed and spoke to him on his way out. Then she nodded to me, indicating the matter was arranged.

As I emerged from the dining room, Clara handed me a pith helmet that had just been given her by Mme. Oberman. It was a little large and I had the feeling I was walking around inside an inverted laundry basket, but it served the purpose.

In the compound not far from where we stood, the Doctor was giving working instructions for the day to perhaps two dozen Africans. First there had been a roll call and now the doctor was dividing the men into different groups, one of which was to collect stray lumber around the place, another of which was to repair the porch on one of the long bungalows occupied by the staff, and still another of which was to carry on the war against the jungle, cutting, pruning, weeding, pushing back. I could readily see the truth of the remark that had been made in connection with Lambaréné, that if you left the jungle to itself for two months, it would close in over you and you would have to tunnel your way out.

Dr. Schweitzer completed his instructions and motioned to Clara and me to follow. He went up the several steps to his quarters, which were at one end of the long bungalow facing the compound. Just to the side of it was a fenced-in area for several antelopes.

The Doctor's room, like all the others, was open at both ends, covered by a wire screen and supporting woodwork. On the far side he had his desk, part of which was under a mound of papers and books. Opposite it was a medium-sized bookcase. The Doctor asked us to be seated, then sat on a stool at least as old as the hospital. I made a mental note of the fact that nowhere at Lambaréné had I seen an upholstered chair or anything even resembling a sofa or couch.

Dr. Schweitzer apologized for the fact that we did not have a talk the previous afternoon. He pointed to a pile of forms on his desk.

"All this is to be filled out," he said. "Now the French government has asked us to prepare complicated forms for each patient at the Hospital. Miserable paper work. Also now we have to fill out workmen's compensation forms for the working people who come to the Hospital. Dozens of items for each patient. And I hardly know what to do with these."

He lifted his head in the direction of one end of his desk, indicating a large bundle of new mail.

"My paper work is killing me," he said slowly. "Week by week the mail gets larger. Mlle. Ali and Mlle. Mathilde help me as much as they can. Even so, we keep falling farther and farther behind. Many of them are important letters which must be answered. Some of them are from theologians who raise significant questions in connection with things they may have read that I had written at one time or another. The least I can do is to try to answer them. I am maybe fourteen months behind with part of my correspondence. Some of the letters involve the work of the Hospital— people who volunteer to work here.

"While the turnover is not excessively large, we do have to bring in new people now and then. The nurses and doctors here have to take a leave of absence after a year or two just to rest up after the exhausting work in this climate. And so new people keep coming. Before a new nurse arrives at the hospital, some twenty-seven letters have to be written. It is important, so very important, to be sure about these things. It is not like a girl coming to the city from the country to get a job. It is a long way from Europe and America to Lambaréné. And the only way I have of finding out what I must know about each person is through letters—most of all the letters the person herself writes, but also what I can learn from other people.

"After it is decided that a nurse or doctor is to come here, then the real work begins. I must be very clear and very complete in the instructions. Passports, visas, en-route accommodations.

"But we will not talk any more about this. Are you comfortable in your quarters?"

I said I was very comfortable indeed. I told the Doctor I was eager to take care of some matters, and handed him the letter from President Eisenhower. He opened the letter carefully, then read it without translation.

"A letter from the President of the United States," he said slowly, then read it again. I could see that he was moved by what the President had written. Then he looked up and smiled.

"Do you know," he said, "that if, eighty-two years ago, my dear mother had been told by someone that her little baby would someday receive a letter from the President of the United States, she would have had the surprise of her life. This is a very kind letter from the President. I will take great pride in returning the greeting."

Then I conveyed the cordial good wishes of Prime Minister Nehru. At the Doctor's request, I told him about the Prime Minister's recent visit to the United States, and the importance attached to it by President Eisenhower. I referred to the fact that in the past few years some misunderstanding had developed between the United States and India. This was not merely a matter of differing foreign policies. Public opinion in both countries had been growing apart. In America, the mistaken notion existed that India had ranged itself on the side of the Soviet against the United States, especially as it concerned the decisions made in the United Nations. In India, a large segment of public opinion took the view that the United States was insensitive to the independence movement in Asia and Africa, and that we were determined to preserve the interests of the colonial powers in that part of the world.

The result of both these views was that the two peoples of the world whose national historical experience had so much in common and who, by standing together, could contribute so mightily in the building of essential bridges between East and West, were drifting apart. Hence the significance of Mr. Nehru's trip to the United States. Both the President and the Prime Minister had developed an instant mutual admiration and respect.

In talking to the Prime Minister before he returned to India, I learned that the exchange of views with the President had cleared up many matters in his mind. At the same time, he was able to impress on the President the reasons for the positions taken by India with respect to affairs in Asia and the Middle East.

The Prime Minister attached the utmost importance to the uprisings in Poland and Hungary. What happened in Hungary,

c. u

"If, eighty-two years ago, my dear mother had been told by someone that her little baby would
me day receive a letter from the President of the United States, she would have had the
irprise of her life . . ."

he said, would have a profound effect everywhere, especially among young people who would now realize that communism could no longer be the headquarters for their natural idealism. And even though the uprisings were suppressed, there would be profound internal changes in the Communist world, he felt, changes that would inevitably move away from the old dictatorial shape of things. People were demanding something better than what they had known; they were demanding greater liberty and a better life. And there was no way for this demand to be resisted. He was therefore hopeful that, given world peace and a little time, there would be long steps forward for a large part of the world community.

Dr. Schweitzer listened carefully. He recalled the time he had met Nehru in Lausanne in 1936. He was impressed by the interesting combination in Nehru of the contemplative man and the man of action. And he was fascinated by the way Nehru complemented Gandhi.

But enough of politics, he said. There was work to be done around the Hospital and he invited me to tag along if I wished.

There was still the matter of Marc Chalufour and his crusade to save the church organ. I decided to bring it up another time. As for the main reasons I had come to Lambaréné—making duplicate copies of the Doctor's unpublished and unfinished manuscripts, and the possibility of direct action by him on the matter of world peace —these would have to wait for an hour when there might be some easing of the pressures of the Hospital. But the more I learned about the Hospital and about Dr. Schweitzer, the more pessimistic I became that such an hour might be found.

In any event, I accepted the Doctor's invitation to accompany him as he discharged his morning chores. The first job we had was to move planks of lumber that had been stored in several places to the porch of a bungalow that was now under repair. The wood was the finest mahogany in the world. Its use as floor boards was dictated by two factors: first, the abundance of mahogany in the general area of Lambaréné, making it inexpensive; second, the need for the hardest woods as protection against termites. Much of the Hospital, in fact, had been built with the kind of hardwoods that in Europe and the United States were reserved for the most costly cabinets or luxury paneling.

The Doctor worked alongside the Africans as the wood was transported by hand and placed in neat piles under the bungalow porch being repaired.

Our next job was to get rid of crates of medicines that had spoiled because they were improperly packed before being shipped. Shippers in Europe and the United States, apparently, have little experience in preparing medicines for storage under equatorial conditions. In addition to the heat and the moisture, medicines have to contend with raiding ants. Large crates would arrive with labels saying they had been specially sealed to guard against heat and moisture; but within three weeks after arriving at Lambaréné they had to be repacked. Even sealed metal drums sometimes failed to do the job. I watched two such drums containing millions of cathartic molasses tablets emptied into wheelbarrows for dumping into the river because they had spoiled or turned into tar.

Then several large packages of aspirin had to be dumped. There was some evidence indicating successful ant raids into the aspirin stores. Judging by the size and activity of the ants at the Hospital, I would have supposed that they were in no need of pain killers. In any event, they kept coming back for more. The ants, who have an appetite for paper, made it necessary to do double labeling on each bottle. In fact, almost everything connected with the medicines required two or three times as much work as it would in a temperate zone. Every bottle, for example, had to be resealed with paraffin after it arrived.

Ideally, of course, a hospital should have large refrigeration facilities for its medical supplies. This is especially true with respect to the new antibiotics. But there was very limited refrigeration equipment at the Schweitzer Hospital. For the most part, the medicines had to be stored in the empty space underneath buildings that were so situated on the hillside that they had relative protection against the sun. Sometimes the Doctor had to get down on his hands and knees and crawl through the dirt in order to check on the medicines and help move them as might be required.

After two hours of working alongside the Doctor I was ready to throw in the towel. The Doctor's shirt was wringing wet. His hair lay in moist gray clumps on his forehead.

Again I had to keep reminding myself that the Doctor was entering his eighty-third year. Just trying to keep up with his stride as he hurried from place to place was a feat of endurance, I could hardly wait for the afternoon siesta.

When I entered the dining room, I felt fully at home for the first time. For I knew that the look of severe midday fatigue on all the faces of the staff was reflected on my own. The Doctor, too, showed the effects of his exertions. Yet it was astounding and wonderful to see the way even a brief respite and a good meal enabled him to recoup his energies. After he had had his soup and was halfway through his cheese and noodles the color began to come back to his face. By the end of the meal he was sitting straight in his chair, his eyes were twinkling, and he had some stories to tell the staff that lifted their spirits.

"I have an announcement to make," he said. "Civilization in all its glory has finally come to Lambaréné. Less than a mile from the Hospital today there was an automobile accident. There are probably only two cars within miles of the place; today they inevitably met in a crash and we treated the drivers for some minor injuries. If anyone here has reverence for automobiles he is welcome to treat the cars."

Then he turned to Albertina.

"How is your pet monkey doing these days?" he asked.

"Not very well," Albertina replied. "I set him free in the morning but he has a terrible habit of wandering too far and has increasing difficulty in finding his way home."

The Doctor smiled. "Maybe he drinks too much," he said.

On my way out of the dining room, I asked Clara when she thought we might discuss with the Doctor the two main purposes that brought us to Lambaréné. She said we might have to wait another day or two, perhaps longer; when the right time came, the Doctor would come to us.

Walking toward my room, I passed the Doctor's quarters. Through the wire screen I could make out his silhouetted form perched over his correspondence. For the rest of the afternoon I stayed in my room, taking care of office matters that had been air-mailed to me from *The Saturday Review* in New York. Like everything else in the world, my job had been revolutionized by the air age. There is hardly a place in the world that cannot be reached by person or mail in forty-eight hours. I have had airmail bundles of work from New York only two and a half days old delivered to me in a Moslem village fifty miles from Dacca in East Pakistan. On another occasion, a postman on a bicycle met me coming out from a small Japanese inn near Nagasaki and handed me page proofs of the forthcoming issue of *The Saturday Review*. And now in a jungle hospital in Africa, I was no farther away from my office than I would have been twenty years earlier in Colorado.

The airplane has made it not only possible but necessary for an editor to move his desk from place to place in the world. Indeed, the airplane itself has become an efficient and productive office. Nowhere outside of a plane have I found such ideal working and thinking conditions. When at my job in New York, my main business each day is to preside over interruptions. I have little time for reading, less time for writing. Sequence is annihilated. One takes things as they come, and they come in short, uneven bursts. Once, I became sufficiently objective about my job to keep track of everything that happened in the course of an average day. I discovered that the telephone rang on the average of once every six minutes; that there were at least six callers each day, three of whom came by previous arrangement; that the important business that had to be transacted with the staff had to be squeezed into less than an hour and a half. In between the telephone and the appointments, I would work on my unanswered-mail folder, which weighed heavily on me even when out of sight. I would type my replies on the back of each letter for retyping by my secretary on office stationery.

On a plane, however, especially when we are high above the clouds, the fragmentation disappears. Sequence comes to life again and the mind has a chance to reorganize itself for consecutive thought. The meal tray serves as an excellent stand for my typewriter and the seat beside me becomes a side table for working papers. I estimate that one hour in the sky office is the equivalent of about four hours on land in terms of actual output.

There are, of course, distractions. The sky itself. Even so, it is the kind of distraction that nourishes thought. For nowhere else in the world is there grandeur like this. Sometimes, when flying above a storm, vast, clearly defined cloud masses catch the light of the sun; the result is a Grand Canyon of color multiplied by infinity. Once, flying from Seattle to San Francisco, I saw three distinct cloud levels, with clear sky in between. Each level had its own character. The first was a massive purple floor, swelling and bulging when we were close to it. The second layer was full of tunnels and canyons, exploiting every gradation of gray and black. The third level abandoned itself to color, with gentle formations suggesting lakes of gleaming silver, or long lemon-colored slopes meeting a light green-blue sky.

Another time, flying from Beirut to Karachi, we darted in and out of vast thunderheads, each of which looked as though it was made up of the combined masses of all the mountains in the world. The thunderheads each ran up to forty thousand feet, growing fatter and more menacing on their way up, and then, suddenly, they flattened out on the top, connecting with each other to make a giant white roadbed. Underneath were the long caverns, deep gray on one side, streaked blue on the other. For more than an hour, we rode through the caverns until we finally hit a long open clearing.

I need not even mention the sunsets. The combination of the setting sun, the winds, and the swift movement of the plane changes the landscape so rapidly that no two minutes are the same. It is a developing wonder and makes a moving picture that stays in the mind. And, if you catch the late sun just right as you fly west, it will cause thin golden threads to spin off the propellers.

As I say, these are nourishing distractions, and I welcome as many of them as I can find. Indeed, I have made a hobby of collecting skyscapes, and now have some two dozen in my memory box to think back upon. It is the kind of hobby that goes naturally with the kind of job that has the world for its locale.

VI

ON MY THIRD MORNING at Lambaréné, after breakfast, I crossed the small compound from the dining room to the porch of the Schweitzer quarters in order to pay my respects to Mrs. Schweitzer. She was seated in a dilapidated beach chair. In her hand was a long bamboo rod which she used to fend off some of the animals that would otherwise disturb her rest. In particular, there was one bird she had to guard against. He looked like a cross between a raven and a parrot. He would come swooping down and alight on your shoulder or the back of your neck. If you weren't used to this sort of thing, it could be somewhat unnerving, for it would happen very suddenly and you hardly knew what hit you. Generally, it would be accompanied by a sudden flapping of wings and occasionally a nip of the ear. This bird was totally gregarious and it was hard to persuade him that his attentions were not always the ultimate in human enjoyment. Mrs. Schweitzer liked to doze in her chair. So long as she held onto the bamboo rod, the bird respected her solitude. But when the rod was absent, the bird invariably interpreted it as an invitation to a shoulder.

The first time I saw Mrs. Schweitzer I could see she was not well. The blue veins stood out in her forehead and seemed stark against the pure whiteness of her skin. She had lovely gray-brown eyes but they seemed to look at you through a mist. When she spoke it was with considerable effort. Her breathing was labored. Despite her difficulties, she would not allow anyone to treat her as an invalid. She insisted on coming to the dining room for lunch and frequently for dinner. It was easy to see how much of a struggle it was for her, even with the aid of a cane, to negotiate the two dozen or so steps across the compound and climb the short stairs to the dining room. Once, I saw Mrs. Schweitzer start out across the compound, her weight bent forward on the cane and her whole being struggling for breath. I rushed to her side and took her arm. She looked up at me, somewhat puzzled, as though I did not know the rules of the game at Lambaréné. Then she smiled and thanked me but said she was in the habit of getting around by herself. She expressed the hope that I might come to visit her on the porch and talk to her.

"You know," she said, "I am so interested, so very much interested, in what is happening in the world, and here one does not often get a chance to talk about it. The Doctor is very busy with the Hospital and all his other work and I do not want to tire him by asking him about things. So there is very little talk. And I am hungry for talk, especially about the world. It would be very nice if you could come to visit with me; that is, if you are not too busy."

I accepted the invitation gratefully. And now, the next day, I visited Mrs. Schweitzer on the porch. She bid me draw up a chair and told me she would do her best to protect me against the bird now making short circles above my head in preparation for a landing.

She apologized for the fact that she was unable to escort me to such parts of the grounds as I might like to see. Many years earlier, she had had a skiing accident that had broken her spine; in recent months she found it increasingly difficult to get around. Hence the cane and her seat on the porch.

"It makes me feel so foolish," she said, "this being so helpless. I ought to be working with the Doctor. He is an amazing man. I really think he is working harder now than he did twenty years ago. And twenty years ago I was afraid he was killing himself with work. He has always said that he has a favorite prescription for anyone over sixty who does not feel well—hard work and more hard work. As you can see, it is a prescription he follows himself.

"I am only sorry I cannot work hard, too. We have been working here a long time . . . more than forty years. I used to be able to help the Doctor; but in the last few years it has no longer been possible for me to do so."

I asked Mrs. Schweitzer which place she considered her real home—Gunsbach or Lambaréné.

"Actually, there are three homes," she said. "When I was young, shortly after I was married, I contracted tuberculosis, so we went to live in the Black Forest of Germany, where the climate was considered helpful for people in that condition. We liked it very much, so very much that we kept a home there even after I was cured.

"Then there is the home in Gunsbach—in Alsace, as you know. At first it was very much a home, but we spent less and less time there. And whenever we returned, there would be so many people who wanted to see my husband that I came to regard it more as an office than a home.

"And so, of the three places, this place seems most like home to me. It is very hot here in Lambaréné; it is very moist and there isn't much more than a bedroom to our own quarters. But this place to me has been our main home for more than forty years."

When I asked about their daughter, Mrs. Schweitzer said that she wasn't sure that Rhena had the same feeling about Lambaréné being a home for her.

"You see," she said, "when Rhena was small, the Doctor did not feel that Lambaréné was a good place in which to bring up a child. And so we sent her to boarding school. In later years, when she was fully grown, she came here for a visit—for a few weeks. She is now married, to Jean Eckert of Zurich, an organ builder, and she of course has her own home."

Mrs. Schweitzer then got up from her chair and went inside.

After a moment she reappeared, holding the family album. One of the early photographs showed the Albert Schweitzers with their little girl. Albert Schweitzer was young and sturdy, with black wavy hair, a thick mustache, and an unwrinkled face. Helena Schweitzer was pretty and vivacious; her features were thin and sensitive but there was great strength and directness in the face. Rhena had large dark eyes and held her mother's hand. She wore the expression so familiar to parents of little girls—part shyness, part curiosity, part uncertainty, part feminine delight in being asked to pose.

Another photograph showed Dr. Schweitzer at the age of thirty-seven or -eight. This was about the time he was getting ready to come to Lambaréné. He was in a reflective mood. His wide-set eyes had caught a distant light and seemed to carry him outside the frame of the photograph. His chin was resting on his closed right hand. There was a quizzical look around the mouth. There was no trace of whiteness in the hair.

Then there was a picture taken of Rhena and her husband just after they were married. Mr. Eckert was alert and well groomed. Right after this were other family pictures of the Eckerts, the most recent of which showed their sixteen-year-old boy, Philippe, who had recently been very ill but who was fast recuperating. Mrs. Schweitzer said the Doctor was very fond of Philippe.

"Here," Mrs. Schweitzer said, "you were interested in our home in Gunsbach. This is a picture of the street and this is a picture of the house itself. It is a nice house, not pretentious, but very sturdy and comfortable.

"I like these pictures. I turn to them very often. Those early pictures were taken so many years ago that it is hard to remember exactly how many. Now we do not take pictures any more.

"I know I am talking like an old woman. But it is true. I am old. I am very old. And now I have very little to do except to look at these pictures and old letters and think back upon our life together.

"You will forgive me? Thank you. I am so eager to hear about your own family. Clara has told me about your wonderful wife and your children—four or five girls, which?"

I took out a small group photograph showing Ellen and three of the four girls. I did not happen to have a picture of the youngest girl.

Mrs. Schweitzer lingered a long time over the photograph, asking me to describe each child. This I did with relish and supporting anecdotal material. Then, at her request, I told her about our home and the openness and sense of freedom it afforded the children. She eagerly devoured the information about my family and made me promise to send additional photographs from time to time.

I feared I might be intruding on her rest, so I got up to leave. She made me sit down again, saying that it had been a long time since she had had the opportunity to talk to anyone so fully. Besides, we hadn't even mentioned the world situation. What about the political situation in the United States? What about the struggle between East and West? What about communism? What about atomic energy?

"You must understand," she said, "that there aren't many visitors from the United States. And those who come do not stay for very long. They have urgent business, or so it seems, with the Doctor, and there isn't much opportunity to talk to them."

For the next hour I answered Mrs. Schweitzer's questions as best I could—and she had comments of her own to make now and then.

"It is so terrible," she said, "the world gets rid of one monster like Hitler but there are always others waiting in the wings to take his place. Isn't it strange? Human beings allow themselves to become all twisted under the influence of these men. I have seen it happen to many people I knew in Germany. I have seen the change that came over these human beings. I have seen decent people turn into killers and sadists."

She was of Jewish origin; she knew what she talked about.

"Anyway, we do the best we can and we work for better things. I don't know why I say 'we.' My time is over. I am too old. But I can hope. No one is ever so old that he cannot hope—even if his hopes are for others. I have done much such hoping in my life—and some of the hopes have come true. In recent years for me there has been not much to do except to hope—and to look at the pictures and think·back."

Mrs. Schweitzer did not come to dinner that night. I feared that our conversation had been a drain on her energies, but Clara told me that she had been coming to dinner with decreasing frequency in recent weeks.

I next saw Mrs. Schweitzer at lunch the following day. She was at least fifteen minutes late in coming to her place. For the longest time after she sat down she had difficulty in getting her breath. Her lips were a stark blue. But she smiled graciously and did her best to engage in conversation. All she had for the noonday meal was a cup of tea. When she got up to leave she beckoned to me. Once we were outside she said she hoped I would visit her again on her porch. It meant so much to her, she repeated, to talk to people who have just come from the United States.

I had several visits with Mrs. Schweitzer while I was at Lambaréné. I came to admire her pride, her resourcefulness, her tenacity, her continuing interest in the outside world.

Two months after I returned from the Hospital at Lambaréné, I picked up a newspaper and learned that Mrs. Schweitzer had died. Her life had not been an easy one, but it had known purpose and hope and grace.

"There is such a thing as being too detached."

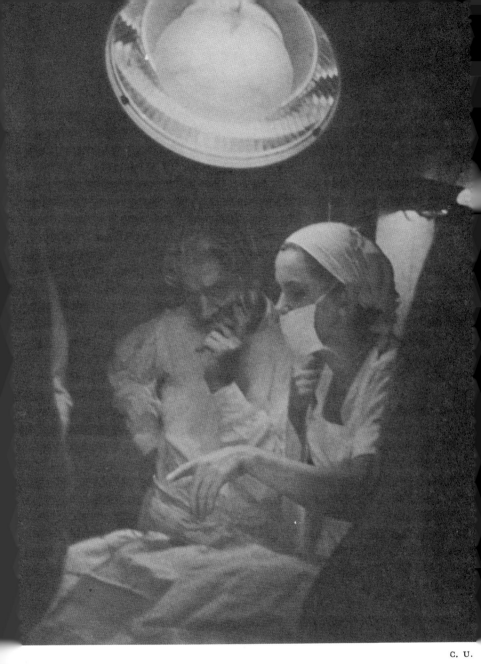

C. U.

ne can't expect philosophers to be romanticists . . . the philosopher must deal not only
h the techniques of reason or with matter and space and stars, but with people."

c

"Goethe became a prisoner of his own promises. I don't want that to happen to me."

VII

ON THE AFTERNOON of my fourth day at Lambaréné, Dr. Schweitzer came to my room and said he hoped it might be convenient for us to talk. He said it would be nice if we could be incommunicado from the rest of the Hospital for about two hours. We found Clara who suggested that we meet in her room which was out of sight from the main Hospital paths.

Dr. Schweitzer seated himself on the bed, his arm resting on the white metal tubing on the lower end. I don't recall how we happened to get on the subject of philosophy, but for at least two hours he discussed his debt to the great thinkers in history.

At one point, he stopped short, saying that one did a disservice to philosophy in general and certain philosophers in particular if one had nothing to offer them except praise. He pointed out, as Bacon and others have done, that the uncritical acceptance of Aristotle for many centuries actually had the effect of retarding speculative and systematic thought. There was a tendency to view Aristotle as the be-all and end-all of philosophy, with the result that hardly anyone felt there was any point in further exploration or development.

"Philosophy will never be complete and can never be complete, by the very nature of philosophy. The human mind is capable of infinite growth. There are endless adventures in creative thought ahead of us. It is only when men bow low before great thinkers and proclaim them to have said the last word that philosophical growth becomes arrested.

"Aristotle wasn't the only one. There was Kant. He was such a giant that men who should be working on the philosophical frontiers drew back and confined themselves to endless interpretations and theorizing about Kant. It was important, of course, for qualified thinkers to analyze Kant, but they had a tendency to make this analysis an end in itself. And since Kant was regarded as the last word, the new words were delayed in coming."

Then Dr. Schweitzer ran his fingers through his long, shaggy hair—one of the most characteristic of his gestures.

"I can't blame all this on Kant, of course," he said. "But I can blame him for being so much system and so little compassion. One can't expect philosophers to be romanticists, but it is important to remember that the philosopher must deal not only with the techniques of reason or with matter and space and stars, but with people. After all, it is the relationship of man to the universe, and not solely the relationship of one galaxy to another, or one fact to another, that should occupy such an important part of the philosopher's quest. There is such a thing as being too detached. I fear this may have been true of Kant."

There were other things in philosophy that bothered Dr. Schweitzer. Philosophical catchwords, for example. The way a phrase would be picked up and used almost automatically whenever a man's name would be mentioned, as though the phrase described the sum total of his life and thought.

He spoke of Descartes.

"One would think that Descartes lived just to emit a line of staggering profundity: 'I think, therefore I am.' How rare are the full-bodied examinations of his work. There has been too much genuflecting before *'Cogito, ergo sum'*; too many philosophical monuments have been erected in its behalf.

"I find it difficult to be impressed by 'I think, therefore I am.'

One might as well say, 'I have a toothache, therefore I exist.' These catchwords are tricky things. I don't think they serve the cause of creative thought in philosophy."

Then he looked up and said, "I have been negative enough. Too negative. There are philosophers whom I like and who have exercised strong influence on my own thought. Hegel, most of all. A man of reason. But also a man with a deep respect for the possibilities of the human being, especially the capacity to embrace important new concepts. Hegel is a philosopher who deserves well the mind concerned with the problems of its own growth.

"As for a school of philosophical thought, I acknowledge my great debt to the Stoics. To my mind it is the greatest formal philosophy in human history. To the extent that I can be identified with any one school, I should be proud to be related to the Stoics. There have been other influences, of course. I have a high admiration for the English philosophers of the late seventeenth and eighteenth centuries. They were imaginative but precise. They were concerned with man's estate.

"I have also found myself influenced by the early Chinese philosophers. There is an intense human quality in their thought. They never allow themselves to get too far away from their speculations about the nature of man or the purpose of man. And it is only logical that out of all this thought should come such a creative naturalism."

Dr. Schweitzer stared at the opposite wall. He said that these real influences in his philosophical thought were sometimes overlooked in the appraisals by others. It would be said, for example, that the Buddhist influence in his work was pre-eminent. This was a mistake.

"The mistake is natural enough," he said. "There is a disposition to think that because I am so deeply concerned with the need for reverence for life that my philosophy must be Buddhist, especially in connection with the Buddhist emphasis on the importance of animal life. But there is much more to Buddhism than that; and I hope there may be more to my own philosophy than that.

"A moment ago I was talking about the need to be careful of philosophical catch phrases. It is true that no single phase of my own philosophy is more representative of my thinking than 'reverence for life.' But the phrase is related to a whole line of thought. Rather than have people speculate on whether this phrase connects me to this philosophy or that, I would have them look into the purpose and the meaning of my work as a whole, such as it is.

"Christian theology has found it difficult to come to terms with my thought, though Christians have not."

He paused as he made this distinction.

"I have the feeling that the Christian theologians are reluctant to come in through the door I have tried to open. I have tried to relate Christianity to the sacredness of all life. It seems to me this is a vital part of Christianity as I understand it. But the Christian theologians, many of them, confine Christianity to the human form of life. It does not seem to me to be correct. It lacks the essential universalization that I associate with Jesus. Why limit reverence for life to the human form? As I say, I have tried to open the door; I hope the Christian theologians will come in."

I asked Dr. Schweitzer whether these philosophical ideas were reflected in the two books I understood were now close to completion.

He replied, yes, these ideas were reflected in the two books, but they were not necessarily the main theme. And he proceeded to describe the two unpublished works. He had published two of four volumes which together he calls *The Philosophy of Civilization*. The last two volumes were not quite completed. They were a continuation of the work which had appeared more than a quarter of a century ago. Another book now in manuscript form would be called *The Kingdom of God*. It would be a fairly short book. It would contain his ideas about Christianity and the reality of the human spirit in general.

"In the early 1930's I was determined to finish the two last volumes of *The Philosophy of Civilization*. But I kept being diverted. We were in a period of considerable building at the Hospital in Lambaréné and I found myself putting off my writing from month to month.

"Then, in 1938, I decided to leave Lambaréné in order to work for at least a year on the books. But even before we arrived in Europe—in fact, while we were crossing the Bay of Biscay by boat—I learned that Adolf Hitler had just made a speech in which he tried to reassure the world that his sole aim in everything he did was peace. The speech was such a patent cover-up that I realized the war was not far off. I put all thoughts of my book aside and concentrated on planning for the Hospital's needs in the event of war. I obtained a large stock of medical and other supplies, knowing that we would be largely cut off from Europe. Then I returned to Lambaréné in order to prepare for the war."

He knitted his craggy brows and I could tell that he was reliving the anxieties of the late thirties, when the heavy clank of the iron heel grew louder and nearer with each passing day.

The war came and only occasionally, late at night, was he able to work on the books. And then, at war's end and in the years that followed, a whole new crop of problems sprang up at the Hospital, resulting in yet other postponements for his serious writing. First of all, he said, additional buildings were needed. Then there was the biggest single new project since the Hospital started—his leper village, built with the money he received from the Nobel Peace Prize. And, of course, his visit to the United States in 1949 in connection with the bicentenary celebration at Aspen, Colorado, of Goethe's birth.

"Interruptions—important interruptions—but interruptions all the same," he said. "I worked for months on the Goethe lectures to be given in America. I worked for almost half a year on the Nobel acceptance speech."

I asked if the original Nobel acceptance manuscript was still available; I felt that any number of book publishers would feel privileged to issue it. Perhaps some of the matter might be adapted for article purposes. In that case *The Saturday Review* would like to put in a bid for the material right now.

Dr. Schweitzer said he had not looked at the material for some time, but would, at a later date, send me a copy. He feared, however, that it might need a great deal of work. And he shuddered when he thought of all the other work that claimed priority. Here he was telling me of the difficulty he was having in finding time to finish his two major manuscripts and now, just in the act of talking about it another book was being mentioned.

"Perhaps I had better do what I can, when I can and if I can, on the *Philosophy* and *The Kingdom*. Even though it has been some years now since I have been able to do any sustained writing on these books, my mind has kept ticking away like an old clock a long time after the key had been lost. The central ideas have been developing in my mind; I have a fairly good idea of what it is I should like to say; now all I need is time to say it."

His reference to time jolted me into the awareness of my own responsibility for having taken up so much of his afternoon. I told the Doctor that there was much I wanted to discuss with him, especially as it concerned his manuscripts; but perhaps we should leave it for another time.

He said he had understood from Emory Ross that I had some mission or other in connection with his manuscripts but the whole thing was very mysterious. He smiled and got up to leave.

"Tomorrow, at four o'clock, I will come here again to Clara's room and we will talk. And the mystery will be no more."

As he walked out the door he turned around and cautioned me to wear my helmet at all times. He said it would take him too long to give me all the reasons why it was necessary for me to do so but he hoped I would take his word for it. I told him that by now I was completely indoctrinated.

After he left, Clara said she had a feeling we would get what we came for. She was deeply pleased to see the Doctor so relaxed.

"It's been a long, long time since he has talked this fully about philosophical matters with anybody. He needs it. It is a busy but lonely life here for him at Lambaréné. Always it is the pressure of the Hospital. And he does not have the chance to exchange ideas in the fields that mean so much to him. He will come tomorrow and we will put the two propositions to him."

BUT AT FOUR o'clock the next afternoon, Dr. Schweitzer did not come. Fifteen minutes later we were in the middle of an equatorial squall. I had a large umbrella and I asked Clara whether I ought to take it to him. Clara said that even though the Doctor had no umbrella and seldom used a raincoat he would not be stopped by the heavy rain. This troubled me and when, at four-thirty, the Doctor had failed to arrive, I put on my raincoat and set off after him with the umbrella.

He was not in his bungalow. I learned that he was out in the rain, looking after a new shipment of medicines, making sure they were in a dry place. When he came to his bungalow and saw me standing there with outstretched umbrella, he shook his head slowly and said he hoped I had not thought he had forgotten our engagement.

We walked together to Clara's room. He took off his helmet, hung it on the bedpost, then seated himself on the bed as he had done the day before, resting his arm on the metal tubing. He started off by lightly scolding the both of us for having thought it necessary to come after him. I exonerated Clara and said I had come to fetch him because of the storm. He put me at my ease at this, saying that even old ducks can shed water.

"Now then," he said, "there are some matters you wish to take up with me?"

There were two such matters, I replied. One of them concerned the manuscripts. It was this that Emory Ross had in mind when he had told him of my coming. The other matter was of a more general nature. I would like to defer it until we had had a chance to discuss the first.

"Very well, then," he said, "let us proceed with the first matter. Emory Ross has asked me to give it my most careful and favorable attention. Judging by the way he mentioned the matter, I almost have the feeling of approaching doom."

His face lighted up with a big smile. This put me at ease. I told Dr. Schweitzer that his friends in America and throughout the world, in fact, were deeply concerned about his unpublished manuscripts. They felt it a matter of the most urgent importance that these works be completed and issued. In this latter connection, I said there was serious apprehension over the physical safety of the manuscripts.

"All right," he said, "we will discuss the manuscripts. So that you will know fully all there is to know about them, I will review the situation as it stands at this moment. As I told you yesterday, there are two unpublished manuscripts. Having mentioned *The Philosophy of Civilization* at our meeting yesterday, we will now discuss *The Kingdom of God*.

"No one has seen this book and I have not talked about it. This book is practically complete. The thesis is that Christianity has veered away from Christ. Christianity has constructed an elaborate dogma but it has not really comprehended that the mission of Jesus was to enable every man to discover the Kingdom of God in himself. Jesus wanted to prepare man for the Kingdom of God; it was his dominant concern. But Christianity, as it has developed, has been more concerned about the forgiveness of sins and the resurrection than it has been about the thing that was closest to Jesus—the fact that mankind must understand the meaning of the Kingdom of God. Jesus did not claim to be the Messiah. He claimed to be none of the things that have been claimed for him. He claimed only to know the reality of the coming of the Kingdom of God.

"There is not much more to say about it. An author is really a poor person to talk about the central ideas in his book."

I asked where the manuscript of *The Kingdom of God* was.

"Right here in a trunk at the hospital," he said.

"When will *The Kingdom of God* be ready for publication?"

"As well ask a hen exactly when she expects to produce her egg. I do not know. There are so many things for me to do here at the Hospital. Everything is changing. Now that the Africans have all become French citizens, our whole relationship to the patients is different. Now there are elaborate forms to be filled out for the administration. Each African who wants workman's compensation has to have detailed information supplied about him.

"Formerly, I would just dash off a short note, sign my name to it, and that was that. Now it's endless. And if I say that a patient has been treated and is ready to go back to work, he may become outraged for he would like to stay away from his job yet get paid for it. Little by little, all the joy is going out of our work."

(I recalled reading that when he first came to Lambaréné, Dr. Schweitzer wrote to his friends in Europe, saying that he wished they could come to see his joy when a patient left for home after being treated at the Hospital—well and smiling.)

"And this is not all," he continued. "There is so much work to be done. Little things that have to be done that no one else will do. Look at that curtain. It should have a rod at the bottom, too, so it won't blow into the room when the wind is strong. I must really get to it.

"A few years ago, I thought that my long-range problems at the Hospital were in the process of being solved. I had a doctor here who could take over and keep the Hospital going after I died. And I felt that I would soon have the time I needed to finish my books. But it became necessary for him to leave—the reasons are long and complicated—and then I had to take the entire burden of the Hospital again. The doctors who are with me now are very good but they are very young and so I cannot relinquish the supervision of the running of the Hospital.

"It takes two years before a doctor is really on his own here at Lambaréné. There is so much to learn that can only be learned by experience. When a doctor first comes out, we have to go through certain stages. They all have the same ideas for bringing in electricity and for doing this thing and that—things that many years ago we had decided against for specific reasons—and one has to be patient."

I remarked that the wonder to me was not that he had been able to write so little but that, under the circumstances, he should have been able to write at all.

"The published writings have turned out to be helpful friends," he said. "As I may have told you earlier, the first buildings at this Hospital were paid for by Johann Sebastian Bach. The royalties from my book on Bach, that is. Who knows, perhaps these other works, if I am able to complete them—remote as this may now appear to be—may be similarly helpful."

I asked if we could revert to his *Philosophy of Civilization*. What led him to conceive of it and write it?

"Just before the First World War," he said, "I received an invitation from the London representative of Harper & Brothers to do a book on my philosophy. I started work on it, finishing it shortly after the end of the war. Then I sent it to Harper's, which apparently lost its old enthusiasm for the project, saying they were very sorry, and they returned it. I guess the idea of a book by anyone with a German background—even a French-speaking German from the Alsace—was not too popular in those days.

"And then I sent the book to my publisher in Berlin. And he, too, had no taste for the manuscript. Finally, I didn't know what to do with it, so I asked my friend Emmy Martin, who was going to Munich, to dispose of it any way she wished—on almost any terms.

"Emmy took the manuscript under her arm one day to a publishing house named Beck. I don't think she knew that Beck was primarily interested in legal books, but she went in anyhow and asked to see Mr. Beck. She was told that Mr. Beck was out but that the bookkeeper would see her. He was Herr Albers. Emmy introduced herself. Her hands trembled as she held the manuscript, and with an air of defeat she said she supposed that there would be no interest in a book on philosophy.

"Herr Albers took the manuscript, leafed through some of the pages and said nothing for ten minutes. Then he said that Emmy couldn't have the manuscript back. He wanted to read the entire thing.

"When Emmy Martin wrote to me that Beck would take my book, I was overjoyed. On my next trip, I went in to meet Herr Albers who was to become my close friend for many years—until his death by suicide during the Hitler regime."

At this point Dr. Schweitzer interrupted himself.

"Are you sure that you are interested in this sort of thing?" he asked.

I assured Dr. Schweitzer that nothing could interest me more.

Dr. Schweitzer looked at me closely, smiled slightly, and said he did not want to seem like a garrulous old man. He continued:

"It was just about that time that Albers had persuaded his associates to publish another very long book, this one by a writer named Oswald Spengler, who gave his work the ominous title, *Decline of the West*. And so now Beck had two non-legal heavy philosophical works on his current list.

"One day, the three of us—Albers in the center, Spengler on one side, myself on the other—were going out to lunch together. And I burst out laughing, and said he reminded me of a butcher out walking with his prime oxen.

"There was much trouble before my book was published. All the money Beck made on Spengler was wiped out by the runaway inflation. And my own book was held up because the printing press had been requisitioned by the government in order to turn out more paper money. Finally the book appeared and I was pleased when I learned that it would be translated into other languages.

"But the *Decline and Restoration of Civilization,* as the book was called, was actually only part of a much larger whole. And it is the last part of this larger work that I have had such difficulty in finding time to work on. Most of my time was spent in building up the Hospital. Then one day, during the early thirties, two doctors who were here at the time came to me and insisted that I work at the Hospital during the mornings only and that the afternoons and evenings I give to my manuscript. It was wonderful. I was able to accomplish a great deal. In fact, I even had time to undertake a collection of various autobiographical papers. And so, *Out of My Life and Thought* was born. It was this book, I am told, that called my ideas to the attention of people who had not heard of me before."

That was how I happened to hear about him, I said. Because of my interest in the organ a friend had sent me a copy of the book in 1938, with a slip marking the chapter on organ building. And I remembered what a pleasant discovery it was to find among the moderns someone who still used the Aristotelian system for exploring a subject. The way Aristotle explained plant life was the way Dr. Schweitzer's chapter on the organ treated the art and science of organ building—what kind of wood to use in the pipes, where to place the organ, where to place the choir, what kind of nave was most suitable—dozens of factors that had to be correlated before an organ was built and installed.

While we were talking about *Out of My Life and Thought* one of the nurses came in to ask a question about some drugs that were needed. He disposed of the matter, then resumed:

"I was saying that after *Out of My Life and Thought* appeared, I began to make interesting connections in many places. I received an invitation to give the Gifford Lectures in Edinburgh, which I accepted. I was glad that I did so, for I worked on the lectures for almost two years and derived much intellectual stimulation from it.

"Then came World War II. You will recall that I told you yesterday that I happened to be on a boat passing through the Bay of Biscay, when I became convinced that the war was near, upon hearing that Adolf Hitler had just assured the world that all he wanted was peace. I then returned to Lambaréné in order to prepare the Hospital for carrying on its work even though it might be cut off from a large part of the world in the war years. I was able during that time to give little sustained attention to my writings. Now I don't know whether I shall ever finish *The Philosophy*."

"How much more work is there?" I asked.

"Once again, the mother hen: I have no idea. There is more

work to do here at the Hospital than ever before. More patients. More new buildings. More letters. And the forms to fill out, of course."

"Where is the manuscript of your third volume of *The Philosophy of Civilization?*"

"It is also here at the Hospital—in my trunk."

It was at this point that I told him that his friends were worried about the condition of these manuscripts. I understood that there were no duplicate copies. There were hazards of fire, flood, decay —any one of a number of things that could happen to his work. We believed that it would be wise to have photograph copies made of the manuscripts. And it was for this purpose that I had come with Clara with special camera equipment that would enable us to have film negatives made of all his unpublished work.

He looked somewhat startled at this.

"It would take many, many hours," he said.

I assured him that his own presence would not be necessary, that Clara and I would team up to carry out the project, and that all that would be needed would be the manuscripts.

He said he would consider this and give his answer the following day.

I moved on to the next point and told him that a publisher in New York had authorized me to offer him an advance against royalties of twenty-five thousand dollars for his manuscripts.

"Two things about this," he said.

"The first is that Goethe taught me a lesson that has become a stern rule. Goethe made the mistake of committing himself to deliver books by a certain date without being absolutely certain that he could fulfill the commitment. It tore him apart. He became the prisoner of his own promises. It affected him deeply. I don't want that to happen to me.

"The second thing is that I have learned from the Niebelungen to keep one's loyalty to one's associates. I already have several publishers in the United States who have worked with me."

This matter was discussed rather fully, and I told Dr. Schweitzer that I felt that at whatever time the manuscript would be ready, we could go to the other publishers and inform them of the particular proposal I had just relayed to him, and receive from them some idea of their own capacities and desires in the matter.

"This, too, I will think about," he said. "But now tell me what the other matter is that you wish to discuss."

I took a deep breath, then plunged in. I approached the question of world peace at its largest, discussing existing world tensions in the context of an age that had available to itself total destructive power. No people and no nation were really secure. And the race for security, inevitable under conditions of world anarchy, had the paradoxical effect of intensifying the insecurity. For the new weapons placed a high premium on surprise. Yet the nations felt they had no choice except the pursuit of military strength in a lawless world.

But far more serious was the fact that man was now able to tamper with his genetic integrity. Through radioactivity he was in a position to pursue and punish the unborn generations. He now had the power to change and cheapen the nature of human life. This was power of an ominous order indeed.

I watched Dr. Schweitzer carefully as Clara, speaking very slowly in German, relayed my message. His eyes were closed and his brows were knit. He sat with his head bent forward.

I asked Clara to emphasize that I realized I was not saying anything that he did not know far better than I. My reason for bringing up the subject was that I felt there was no one in the world whose voice would have greater carrying power than his own.

When he asked what it was that we would have him do, I said we had nothing specific to suggest other than that he might feel free to express his concern to the world.

At this moment, Dr. Margaret rapped on the door. She apologized for interrupting but there was an emergency case—a woman with an extrauterine pregnancy who had just been brought to the hospital. An immediate operation was necessary but the woman was already too weak to undergo surgery.

Dr. Schweitzer stood up to leave.

"*La Doctoresse* has come at just the right time," he said. "It is good to be reminded now and then that even in a world struggling with the momentous issue of war and peace the individual has problems.

"We will talk further."

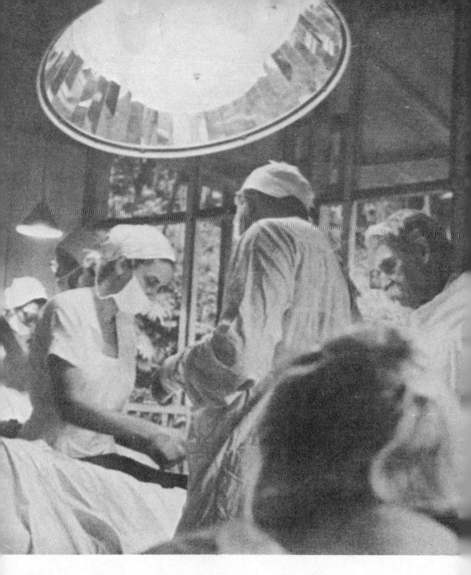

The operating room at the Schweitzer Hospital. Power for the electricity is furnished
generator. The rest of the Hospital is illuminated with oil lamps.

A young African mother in a pensive mood while waiting for her baby to be examined.

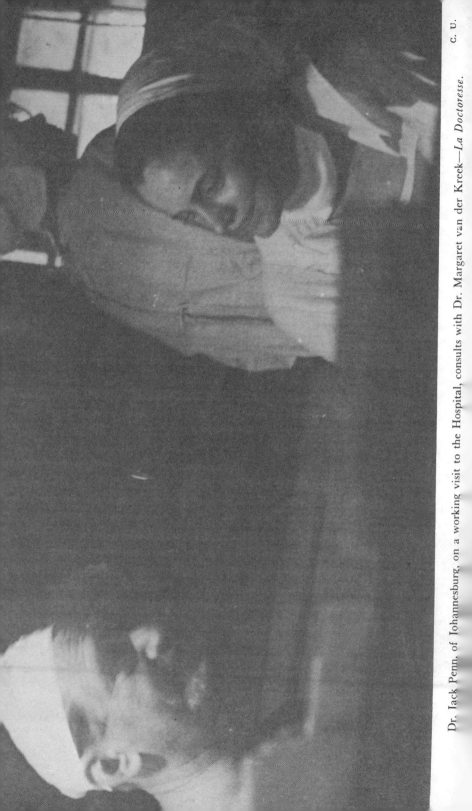

Dr. Jack Penn, of Johannesburg, on a working visit to the Hospital, consults with Dr. Margaret van der Kreek—*La Doctoresse.*

VIII

THERE IS ONLY one place at the Schweitzer Hospital where electricity is available. This is the operating room, where there are modern overhead surgical theater lights. The electricity is furnished by a generator. When the motor is turned on, the throbbing noise alerts everyone that the operating room is going into action. During the night, an African medical orderly is assigned to the river landing. When an emergency case arrives and it appears that surgery may be necessary, he switches on the noisy generator. The effect is that of a gong in a fire station. Doctors and nurses swing out of their beds like firemen, jump into their clothes, and do everything except slide down a brass pole.

Not long after midnight on the day Dr. Margaret came to Clara's room to tell Dr. Schweitzer about the woman with the extrauterine pregnancy, the generator started up. Instantly, I could hear activity in some of the rooms. There were hurried footsteps on the porch. The steady throb of the generator continued for perhaps an hour and a half, or two. Then the motor stopped and after a while I could hear the shuffling footsteps on the porch of the doctors and nurses trudging back to their rooms. I didn't need the sounds to tell me how exhausted they must have been. It was 4:30 A.M. In another two hours the Hospital would be starting on another day. I wondered how many on the staff were too tired even to sleep. The air was heavy and the act of breathing was almost a conscious one. Little wonder that Dr. Margaret, for all her loveliness, showed darkness under her eyes and at times seemed to walk with a stoop. She was no different from the others; fatigue was their constant companion.

About a half hour after the doctors and nurses returned to their quarters, I heard strange voices coming up the hill. At first, the sound was a low rumble. Then, all at once, the voices, now sharp and insistent, seemed to be collected at the end of the porch. These were African voices and they were angry. I got out of bed quickly, put on my khaki pants, and went out on the porch. Not far away in the dim light I could make out some two dozen people in a cluster.

I walked toward the group and perceived the small, slight form of a person who was apparently saying something to the Africans in subdued tones. It was Clara. One of the Africans had stepped forward and said that the group wanted *La Doctoresse* to produce the body of the woman who had just died on the operating table. They had been instructed by the witch doctor to obtain the body in accordance with their customs.

In a voice that indicated understanding but also strength, Clara said that *La Doctoresse* was sleeping; she was exhausted from her night's work. Under no circumstances should she be awakened. Then Clara stepped down from the porch and approached the tall African who was spokesman for the group. For a second I feared for her safety—but only for a second. Clara was saying something to the tall African that caused him to nod, then turn around and speak to the group in a native tongue. There was a brief exchange, but the voices became increasingly moderate, and then the tall African said something to Clara, politely and almost in a whisper, and turned away and started down the hill. The others followed him.

Clara sat down on the steps. I could tell from the way she did it that she had spent herself emotionally. I know she didn't want to talk about it, so I said nothing and went back to my room.

Later, at breakfast, sitting next to Dr. Coulon, I learned what had happened.

The woman had been brought into the Hospital late the previous afternoon. The case had instantly been diagnosed as an extrauterine pregnacy. That is, fertilization had taken place outside the uterus. The embryo had been allowed to develop long past the danger point. Apparently the woman's parents had insisted on witch-doctor treatment, but when the pain became fiendish, the woman's husband took the matter into his own hands, put his wife into a pirogue, and paddled thirty miles to the hospital.

Dr. Coulon said that all the doctors had agreed on the need for an emergency operation to save the young woman's life. But the woman had lost so much blood by the time she had arrived at the Hospital that *La Doctoresse* felt any immediate surgery would almost certainly kill her. Under the circumstances, they decided on immediate transfusions in the hope that the patient might regain sufficient strength to endure an operation.

At about 2:00 A.M. it became clear that the decision to operate could be put off no longer. The embryo had ruptured and an immediate operation became mandatory, however small the chance for success.

La Doctoresse did the operation assisted by the others. The patient died during surgery. It had affected *La Doctoresse* deeply.

"After something like this, it is natural that a doctor should torture himself with doubts," Dr. Coulon said. "Would the patient be alive if we had operated earlier? Perhaps we should not have operated at all? Was there something that should have been done that hadn't been done? I know that *Doctoresse* did everything possible, but I know how she feels."

This sort of experience was not new to Dr. Coulon. He had studied graduate medicine at the Union of South Africa. Then he became an itinerant jungle doctor. He worked in the African villages. The only apothecary available to him was what he carried in his bag. Surgery would generally be performed in the open, on a flat board.

When he arrived at Dr. Schweitzer's Hospital, he marveled at the facilities.

"People come here from New York and are appalled at the crudeness and the startling lack of modern sanitation and instrumentation," he said. "When Mrs. Coulon and I came to the Hospital after working in the open jungle, it was as though we had come into a fairyland. It was wonderful. There was a ward in which patients could be kept under observation. There was a good supply of modern medicine, including the newest antibiotics. There was an operating theater, with overhead electric spot. There was a wide variety of operating instruments. I couldn't have been happier."

I asked Dr. Coulon about the mortality statistics at the Hospital. He said that the mortality might be high by Western standards, but that one had to keep in mind that a larger number of the serious cases had been brought to the Hospital too late for effective medical or surgical care.

All this time we had been conducting our conversation at the breakfast table in very low voices. The death of the young woman after such a long fight to save her had darkened the spirits of the staff. Even Dr. Schweitzer, who ordinarily could be counted on to keep a mood from becoming too heavy, remained silent through the meal. Dr. van Stolk and Dr. Friedmann came in late for breakfast. Neither had shaved. The Doctor nodded to them; they ate quickly, saying little.

After breakfast, on the way back to our quarters, Clara spoke to me about the incident earlier in the morning on the end of the porch. She had been awakened by the voices and she had intercepted the group before they could get to La Doctoresse's room. The Africans lived in the constant presence of death. Even so, its mysteries gave birth to many dictates and rituals. And one never knew at the hospital when the fact of sudden death would cause a group to act in an inexplicable and apparently hostile way.

I asked what she had said to the group to cause it to turn back. She said she had tried, as simply and sincerely as she could, to give them some idea how Dr. Margaret and the others had fought to save the young woman's life.

"I told them that only *La Doctoresse* had the authority to release the body," she said, "and that when she did so she would turn it over to a member of the family as was the custom, and not to a crowd. For if the body were turned over to a crowd every time it asked for it, people would lose their confidence in the Hospital staff. I said I was certain the tall African could see this.

"These are basically very kind people and they respond to kindness," she continued. "Somehow they had gained the notion that the young woman had been sacrificed in some way or another. I knew if I could make them see how Dr. Margaret had given of herself to save the young woman, and how unkind it was to make demands on her now that she had finally earned some rest, they would change their minds. The leader of the group must be a very fine man; just before he left he said he was sorry that they had awakened me and sorry that the group had wanted to disturb *La Doctoresse*. As I say, these are wonderful people."

Just before we came to our bungalow, we met George Malthen, with whom I had had a talk some days earlier and who had brought his wife to the Hospital against the orders of the local fetisher. He said his wife was now well again, thanks to Dr. Margaret and the other doctors. They would be leaving for their village directly and he wanted to say good-by.

I thanked George Malthen and we made our farewells.

When we came to the end of the porch, Dr. Margaret was working in her little flower enclosure. She looked up at us and smiled and said how happy she was that two more of her jungle flowers had just bloomed.

Neither Clara nor I referred to the events of the night and early morning. I think that both of us, without saying anything about it, were marveling at Dr. Margaret's ability to become absorbed in the miracle of new life and growth and to have it nourish her at a trying time. She had apparently rested well, brief though it was, and now she was ready to face the Hospital again.

Albertina van Beek Vollenhoven, nurse and ministerial assistant to Dr. Schweitzer. "My doubts no longer seem so terrible."

"A litter on which an object of human size was wrapped in ferns and large leaves."

A young African woman carrying a baby walked up to Dr. Margaret. There was a slight hesitation in her manner but it was obvious she, had something to say.

Dr. Margaret put her at ease. Then the mother exclaimed that her baby was all well again and she was eager to have *La Doctoresse* share her joy.

Dr. Margaret took the child and cradled him in her arms and held him close. He couldn't have been more than six or seven months old.

I had no way of knowing what had been wrong with the baby; but I was glad that the incident had happened just then and in just this way. I also thought of George Malthen's wife. The scales were being balanced; it couldn't have happened at a better time.

Dr. Margaret handed the little boy back to his mother, then turned to us and said she was going down the hill to release the woman's body to the family, so that it could be brought back to the village for burial in accordance with tribal customs.

I went back to my room to take care of some more work that had been mailed to me by the office. But I couldn't put my mind to it. I was thinking of the hospital and of the young people who had come there to help Dr. Schweitzer. I wondered whether they had been prepared for the drama that was waiting for them—for the pain of occasional defeat and the constant challenge of unpredictable human response. Life at the Schweitzer Hospital involved much more than the glamour of being associated with one of the great figures in history. It meant hard work, fatigue, heartbreak. All this came with the decision to be a doctor, of course; but there was an extra dimension at Lambaréné that was almost beyond anticipation.

And what about the Africans themselves? How did they feel about the young men and women in white who had a method of treating them and their families far different from the treatment their own customs sanctioned or dictated. Why, when death occurred, was there such a powerful tug of reversion? Did they regard this inability of a white doctor to save a black life as proof of the fallibility of the white man, and as punishment for the Africans for having wandered outside that which was part of them?

I looked out the screened door and saw a small procession in single file led by Albertina going up the hill. Mme. Oberman was walking behind Albertina, followed by two Africans carrying picks and shovels. Behind them two Africans were carrying a litter on which an object of human size was wrapped in ferns and large leaves.

I put down my work and followed the procession along the narrow path leading up the hill toward the leper village. A little more than halfway toward the village, Albertina led the procession on a path off to the right. Very shortly we came to a clearing; it was a burial ground for those persons who had died at the hospital and had no relatives or friends to claim them. In accordance with the custom of the Africans who lived in this part of the Continent, the dead are carefully wrapped in long ferns before they are laid to rest.

Two Africans were at work preparing the grave. Their picks and shovels cut easily into the soft rich ground. Albertina and Mme. Oberman stood off to one side. When the grave was ready, Albertina read from the Bible while the body was put to rest. She continued the prayers for several moments and closed the book. Then the Africans filled in the grave again, working steadily. When they were through, they looked up at Albertina who said a final prayer. Then we walked in single file down the narrow path again.

As we neared the bungalow and the path widened, Albertina waited for me to catch up with her. She told me that the man who had just been buried had been deranged and had been put in an isolation cell. For days he had refused to eat, yet there was something about him that Albertina liked and admired. So far as anyone knew, he was alone in the world. He had come to the Hospital on his own, unusual for a mental case. As his condition became progressively more acute, he seemed to know that he had come to the right place. He would have periods of agony and violence, which necessitated his isolation, but he would also have moments of apparent clarity.

Only the previous evening, when Albertina came to look after him, she found him in a rational and quiet mood. He beckoned to her and told her that he thought he was going to die. He reached out and took her hand and said he was grateful to her for taking such good care of him. Then he lapsed into silence for a long time. Albertina could tell he was slipping. After a few moments he said in a low voice that he had always feared that he would be alone when he died. But now he was not alone because of Albertina, and he was content and grateful.

He asked Albertina to pray for him, which she did. Before she was through, he passed away.

And now, on the way down the hill again, Albertina was telling me about the man.

"Sometimes I wonder," she said, "whether my coming here makes sense—whether I am doing anything that is really useful. Then something like this happens, and my doubts no longer seem so terrible."

In the days that followed, I was to learn that Albertina fulfilled a dual role at Lambaréné—nurse in charge of the psychiatric ward and ministerial assistant to Dr. Schweitzer.

There was no chapel at Lambaréné. Sunday services were held in the open air. The Sunday I was there I was directed to the long, narrow compound in front of the Hospital clinic. The Africans sat on the steps or in the doorways of the small wooden structures in order to get the protection of the shade. Albertina stood in the hot sun; she wore her customary white pith helmet. During most of the service she read from the Bible. There were a few hymns and the voices of the small African choral group off to one side were heard above the rest.

Like everything else in Lambaréné, the services were simple but effective. After Albertina gave the final benediction, the Africans chatted with each other. A number of them were dressed in their

Sunday best: several men wore long pants and clean shirts, instead of the customary shorts and frayed undershirt. The women, for the most part, wore colored cotton dresses and their hair was neatly done.

Albertina exchanged pleasantries with the people who went up to her after the services. Then she walked slowly up the hill to her room. I watched her until she disappeared from view. Here was a young woman of about twenty-eight or thirty, tall, slender, attractive, intelligent, compassionate. She had defined a mission for herself in life. It was not an easy one. It involved a constant drain on her energies—physical, mental, emotional. Her satisfactions were centered in her exertions. Most of what little time she had to herself she spent in study—reading intensively in the field of mental disease and psychiatric treatment.

And the more I thought about Albertina and the other young people on Dr. Schweitzer's staff, the more I realized their importance and the greater was my admiration. For it took purpose of a very high order to work at Lambaréné. The glamour of the work, such as it is, eventually fades. Those who came expecting to spend most of their time communing with Dr. Schweitzer, or working valiantly alongside him, soon discovered that Lambaréné was no playground for the human spirit. The contact with the Doctor, except at mealtime, was necessarily brief. For the most part a staff member was on his own—that is, if he did a competent job. If not, the Doctor stepped in and attempted to set him straight. Then, if his work was still substandard, the Doctor might switch him to something else. He didn't waste time on idle flattery or trying to keep up appearances; there was too much that had to be done, too little time to do it. More than a few people never made the grade at Lambaréné and came limping home.

That is why Dr. Schweitzer tried to be so careful in screening applicants—why it required a prolonged exchange of letters and detailed checking before a person joined the staff. As a result, an extraordinarily high percentage of the people who came to Lambaréné stayed for years.

Some of the staff members, for example, had served for a quarter-century or more. To be sure, not all of them made their acquaintance with Dr. Schweitzer by mail. A few knew him in Europe and followed him to Africa to serve in any way he wished them to. Mlle. Mathilde Kottman, general supervising assistant who has a total dedication to the Doctor, came to Lambaréné from Alsace about 1923. Mlle. Ali Silver, from Holland, general secretary and personal assistant to the Doctor, and who helped to translate letters from and into English, had served the Doctor for over ten years. Mme. Oberman, who was in charge of billeting, had worked with Dr. Schweitzer on and off for forty years. Mme. Emma Haussknecht, who died in 1956, was the second person to join the Schweitzers at Lambaréné.

While I was at the Hospital, considerable excitement attended the departure of one of the nurses, Maria Langendyk; she had served at the Hospital for sixteen years. And now she was leaving for a rest in Europe. She had completed the term of service she had set for herself.

When I walked into the dining room on the evening before Maria's departure, I could tell that something special was happening. Dr. Schweitzer was wearing his black clip-on tie; some of the younger nurses were wearing lipstick; and there was butter on the table. Clara told me about Maria, a tall woman of about forty-five, with dark hair, dark eyes, and a face of quiet strength. Maria had come to the Hospital, as did the others, asking nothing except the privilege to serve. But her service was now coming to an end. She had spent almost one-third her life with Dr. Schweitzer. This dinner was now in her honor.

Halfway through the meal, just outside the window on the far end of the room, a choral group began to sing. It was a passage from Handel's *Messiah*. The choir was most unusual in the range of its voices. I was able to pick out perhaps a dozen children's voices and the voices of perhaps eight or ten grownups, some of which were deep and strong. The singing was superbly blended.

Clara whispered to me that the voices belonged to African lepers and that they had been trained by Trudi Bochsler, the young nurse in charge of the leper village about a third of a mile from the main body of the Hospital. They had now come to serenade Maria and wish her Godspeed.

I was profoundly impressed by the singing and told Clara so. She said she hoped she might be able to persuade Trudi to have these same lepers put on a repeat performance of the Nativity Play that had so captivated the staff when it was produced at Christmas.

The next morning, virtually the entire Hospital turned out to wave good-by to Maria as she left by pirogue. I saw Trudi, holding a small leper child by the hand, standing not far from Dr. Schweitzer, on a bank overlooking the dock. Dr. Schweitzer was standing in his most characteristic manner—his head forward and his hands folded behind his back. Dr. Friedmann, standing close to Dr. Schweitzer, was waving his helmet as the pirogue carrying Maria slid away from the dock. Perhaps a dozen others rounded out the tableau, as the pirogue, aided by the swift current, eased downstream. I remember thinking that the group on the bank would have made the ideal subject for a mural symbolizing the Schweitzer Hospital.

On the way back from the dock, Clara spoke to Trudi about the possibility of having the lepers do another performance of the Nativity Play. Trudi was delighted by the suggestion and said she was certain that the members of the cast all remembered their parts and would welcome the opportunity to play before the people who hadn't been at the Hospital during Christmas.

Trudi herself was clearly excited about the prospect. Her large gray-blue eyes sparkled as she anticipated the joy that the idea of a repeat performance would bring to the lepers. It would take no time at all, she said, to prepare the production. Perhaps it could be done as early as the following afternoon. Since our next meeting with the Doctor was to be in the evening, the suggestion seemed ideal.

As I got to know Trudi, I was to learn that nothing was more characteristic of her than her spontaneous enthusiasm and sense of immediacy for things that were worth doing. She was open and direct in her dealings with people; no one who knew her entertained any doubts about her intentions or purposes. Nor did she hesitate for a single second to put up a battle for her point of view concerning the operation of the leper village.

Two years earlier Trudi had had a disagreement with Dr. Schweitzer on an administrative matter regarding the leper village. Unable to persuade the Doctor, she left the Hospital and returned to her native Switzerland. For the next six months, neither Trudi nor Dr. Schweitzer rested easily about her departure. Then she wrote to him, asking whether she could return. Though Dr. Schweitzer had strongly espoused his own viewpoint, he was big enough to tell Trudi he was glad she would return and that she could administer the village in accordance with her own ideas.

Trudi returned to Lambaréné at once. While she had been away, she had put each minute to good use, studying every book she could find on the subject of leper colonies. In fact, there was very little that had been published on lepers—whether with respect to medical treatment or their social problems—that Trudi had not read. Her nurse's training had been of a general nature. When she had come to the Hospital for the first time, and she had started to work with the lepers, she went at it as though it would become her lifework. This combination of day-by-day experience and observation and her constant study had now made her, as Dr. Friedmann had remarked, one of the best-informed and most competent persons on the subject in the world.

When Trudi returned to the Hospital she resumed her work with the enthusiastic devotion that is basic in her personality. Increasingly, Dr. Schweitzer tended to give her autonomy in the administration of the village. She became general manager, nurse, interne, teacher, confidante, minister, and family head. And she was getting good results. It was fascinating to see Trudi at work. The lepers worshiped her as though she were their queen, which in many ways she was. She was directly concerned not only about their physical

148

but their emotional well-being. Their trust in her was absolute. When she prescribed a certain routine of medical treatment at the leper clinic, they would accept it without question.

Trudi's only real difficulties were with the witch doctors who hovered just outside the village. Once, when Trudi discovered that some of the patients were not taking their medicines because of omens cast by a witch doctor, she tracked down the fetisher and threatened right then and there to wreak all sorts of havoc on him if he didn't remove his hex at once. The fetisher lost no time in notifying the patients that it was proper and necessary for them to resume their medication.

This young white goddess looked the part. She was twenty-four or twenty-five, flaxen-haired, slender, attractive, intense, inexhaustible. It was clear that her work was giving her the kind of fulfillment she sought in life. She was responsible for the education of the leper youngsters, and each morning she conducted classes and arranged for the purposeful use of the children's time during the afternoon when she had to attend to her medical duties.

When Trudi proposed to her lepers that they put on a performance of the Nativity Play for the visitors at the Hospital, they responded with gleeful anticipation, as she knew they would. Getting up the production for the following day was not an easy undertaking—the costumes had to be located and repaired; the stage props had to be put in order; each person had to brush up on his part; and there had to be a complete rehearsal. But Trudi's certainty that the project was well within their reach was shared by all those who had a part in the play.

The next afternoon, I joined Clara, Dr. Frank Catchpool, and the staff members who were eager to see the play again. We walked down to the leper village. The compound in front of the leper clinic had been transformed into an open-air theater. There were several rows of benches, one of which was already filled with visitors from the Catholic Mission across the river. Back of the benches were perhaps two dozen young African girls from the Mission who had come to pay their respects. They comprised a

The cast.

NES FROM THE NATIVITY PLAY, ACTED AND SUNG BY LEPERS AT THE SCHWEITZER HOSPITAL.

Mary and the infant Jesus.

The audience (from a world of total options).

The audience (lepers; no options).

choir and were to sing during the intermission and at the end of the play.

At the sides of the compound, sitting on benches or on chairs or on the ground, were the lepers. Some of them had bulky bandages on their feet. Others had crutches stretched out alongside them. Even without the bandages and the crutches, the effects of the disease were clearly visible. Toes or fingers were missing, or the feet would be stubbed. A little boy of about ten whose foot had been amputated several weeks earlier went hopping around as he helped put the props into place.

Within five minutes after the play began, a spell of magic settled over the compound. The singing of the actors was full of life and conviction. Two or three of the leper voices had excellent depth and tone. The costumes were crude, very crude, but they helped to create the necessary illusion. The baby Jesus was beautifully behaved, and did not cry until the intermission, and then only briefly. The Three Wise Men were very deliberate in their roles. The leper who took the part of Joseph was compassionate and gentle in his interpretation. Mary obviously relished her role and sang with vigor.

And all the time the play was unfolding, Trudi sat off to one side, her hands clasped and held close to her chest. Her mouth moved in the manner so well known to prompters.

If I say that the entire experience was almost beyond awareness or comprehension, what do those words suggest? Can they possibly indicate the range of emotion or the stretches of thought produced by watching condemned people give life to a spiritual concept? The play was concerned, essentially, with the triumph of hope through faith; but the brief moment of the lepers in a glittering spiritual universe was surrounded on all sides by the evidence of a closed-in world. Yet in that brief moment, they were connected to the things that meant life for most people.

There was something else. The play, in a sense, was almost a symbol of forgiveness. For the white man in Africa had not, in the main, been a friend. Historically, he had not been a liberator or a

Trudi and Dr. Frank Catchpool tend a nature-study class for leper children.

Leper children rehearse for the production of the Nativity Play, under director-prod‧ Trudi Bochsler.

benefactor. He had used his superior knowledge and power to capture the Africans and impress them into slavery. He had brought with him venereal disease. He had caused the African women to bear children and then he had discarded the mothers and their young. He had advertised a religion of mercy and compassion but there had been little of either in his manner. While I watched the lepers at Trudi's village in the Nativity Play, I became conscious of the fact that the play was saying something about a world large enough to hold both black and white. This was close to the original purpose of the play, but original purpose in religion is not too often a remembered part of life. The actors, however, clearly seemed to reflect this original purpose, to which forgiveness belonged.

All this was possible because we were in a segment of Africa where there was a Trudi and an Albert Schweitzer and a Dr. Margaret and an Albertina and a Dr. van Stolk and a Dr. Friedmann and all the others who rescued their whiteness from the evil that the others had spawned.

To the lepers who were on the sidelines, the spotlight for them frequently moved from the actors to the white audience. Comparatively, the poorest among us were rich as kings alongside an African, for we were in a place where wealth was measured by a pair of shoes or an extra pair of pants or an unfrayed blanket. And the lepers heard that we had come from an unbelievable world where people lived in beautiful dwellings of more than one room and could turn a knob that would produce water right in the house, and another knob that would control several fires for cooking. And, miracle of miracles, they saw that education for everyone in the white world was free. There are now schools for the blacks in French Equatorial Africa, of course, but these were mainly in the large cities. And the schools didn't go as far or teach as much as every white child was able to get.

There was nothing resentful in the gazes of the African lepers as they watched us. From their vantage point, we were the main show. The imaginative play of their minds was directed to us rather than to the actors. We probably touched off all sorts of wonderment

Trudi Bochsler, nurse in char
of the lepers, makes her mor
ing rounds of the leper villag
located about one-third of
mile from the main body of t
Hospital.

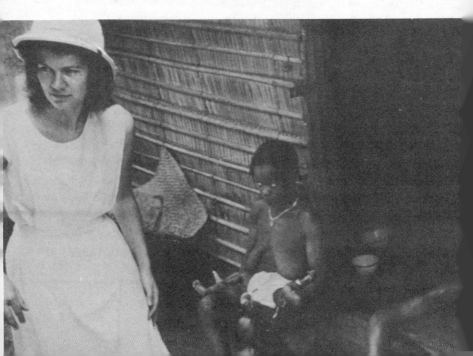

and speculation, especially for the children. Nothing is stranger to the eye of an African child than a white person when seen for the first time. The lack of color creates an aspect of ghastly pallor. It is as though layer after layer of skin had been stripped away, producing what Africans generally refer to as a "peeled" look. The thinness of the facial features of a white person gives him a pinched, closed appearance. I could almost feel the scrutiny of the African children near me.

After the play ended, we sat still for a few minutes. I had no way of knowing whether the same thoughts that had preoccupied my mind were being shared by the others; in any case, the other white visitors sat quietly. They seemed far away in their thoughts. Then the children's choir from the Catholic Mission sang for a few minutes.

We got up to leave. Trudi announced that the leper children had a surprise for us. They had made gifts for each of us—hand-carved letter openers or ship models for the men and beads or pendants or necklaces for the women. Each child had a little presentation speech to make in French; he said he hoped we had enjoyed the play and that we would come to visit the village again.

LET ME DIGRESS a moment.

I suppose people will ask: Is it safe to touch things handled or made by lepers? Is it safe to shake their hands or get close to them?

I have heard much conflicting medical testimony on the subject. Modern theory tends to support the view that leprosy is somewhat akin to tuberculosis and that there are varying stages and degrees of contagion. If the leprosy involves the muscles or nerves, it is not believed to be infectious. If it involves the skin, however, especially where open sores are concerned, then there is the possibility of contagion. Lepers who have lost fingers or toes are in this category. Inflammation of the nasal mucosa with consequent discharge can be a source of infection. Children contract the disease through constant intimacy with leprous members of their families.

Generally speaking, however, outsiders who are in good health are not considered to be in any danger as the result of casual contact with lepers.

It goes without saying that Dr. Schweitzer and his staff expose themselves constantly, regardless of the virulent condition of some lepers. But Dr. Schweitzer is careful to the point of seeming over-cautious in his policy about visitors. He advises them not to get too close to the leper patients and not to shake their hands or touch them. The reason, of course, is that he feels a total responsibility where any risk, however small, to outsiders is involved.

It isn't always easy, however, to follow the Doctor's admonitions. When the little leper boy who handed me the hand-carved letter opener also offered me his hand, I did not see how I could turn away.

On the occasion of another visit to the leper village, a leper introduced me to his wife who was carrying a baby boy of perhaps twenty months or two years. The father told me his child was leprous, too. The baby's nose was running and he had sores all over his face. As I chatted with the parents, the baby twisted in his mother's arms and reached out for me to take him, which I did. To do otherwise, under the circumstances, would have been awkward and indeed impossible.

In general, if you want to see something of Asia or Africa—which is to say, if you want to get close to the people—you would do well to leave your apprehensions behind and take the plunge. If you are in good health, you will have little to fear. Now and then, of course, you are apt to find yourself in delicate situations where a few uneasy thoughts may cross your mind. Once, in a grove not far from Calcutta, I came across a crying child of three or four who was obviously feverish. I carried the child to the nearest village compound. There I learned that the child's parents had died several days earlier, the victims of a smallpox epidemic still raging that had decimated the population of the village. I turned the child over to one of the older women. Certainly it oc-curred to me that I was in an exposed situation; but I tried to take some comfort at least in the fact that I had been inoculated against the disease.

This is not to say that I have been totally immune to infection or illness while abroad. I think I have sampled every species of dysentery recorded in the annals of medicine. I have had to make numberless, unscheduled, and speedy departures from receptions or social functions or public platforms all the way from Djakarta to Mexico City. There were times on the lecture platform in universities in Asia when I was certain I was capable of setting new records for the short sprint and I desperately longed for nothing so much as the chance to prove it. At such times, philosophical calm seems only vaguely attainable and, in fact, quite academic.

On occasion, I fear I may have made a washed-out impression on my hosts. At the University of Yokohama some years ago, for example, I was having dinner at the home of a professor of medicine. I was in my third week of dysentery, having just come from Indo-China. I was as diligent as possible in making it appear that I was enjoying the meal.

All this time my host was observing me closely. Then, at the end of the dinner, he asked to examine my hand. He scrutinized it carefully but dispassionately, as though it were so much disembodied flesh. Then he put his head close to mine and peered into my eyes. His manner became increasingly grave. Finally, he shook his head and said something in Japanese in a low voice to a fellow professor sitting next to him. This gentleman shook his head in turn and passed the word along to another colleague. Soon almost everyone at the table was nodding apprehensively. I felt like a prime exhibit in a surgical theater.

I asked the man at my right what it was that the professor had seen in my hand and in my eyes that had apparently made him so sad. My companion replied that the professor could tell at once that I was dying from cancer. When I inquired about the time factor, I was told that I had at least six months. That was in 1949.

In defense of the professor, it should be said that he had seen me under misleading circumstances; I had had a fairly prolonged adventure in non-retention and no doubt I looked even worse than I felt. It did not seem to him that what was bothering me could be anything short of the worst.

Five years later, I saw the professor again in Tokyo. He had come to call on me at my hotel but I was out at the time—in the public park across the street. Some students had read in the newspapers that I had once played some baseball and they had invited me to join them in a game. The hotel clerk had informed the professor where I might be found. I happened to be on second base when he caught my eye. One of my teammates hit safely and I sprinted for home plate, arriving just ahead of the throw. It occurred to me as I did so that the professor must have thought my ghost was doing the running. It was also true that this was the only time the professor had seen me run when I exercised some option in the matter.

Afterward, when we spoke, he made no reference to his earlier forecast. We discussed various matters. He was eager to come to the United States. He said he had some ideas about medical diagnosis he was eager to put before his professional colleagues in America, and wanted my advice about arranging such meetings. I gave him such help as I could, though I was not unmindful of the fact that I was something less than the perfect advertisement for his theories.

This digression, of course, is touched off by a consideration of the inevitable questions generally asked by prospective travelers about the personal health factor. Generally speaking, the risk while traveling is extremely small. Such deviations as occur are more the result of sudden changes in one's living routine than of basically unhealthy situations. Just the business of adjusting to severe time changes can be constitutionally unsettling. The pursuit of new foods is a delightful adventure; when carried to unreasonable lengths, it can produce deceptively intense but fortunately temporary discomforts.

Experiences such as these, of course, are not peculiar to Americans abroad. They apply equally to visitors to our own shores. The foreign visitor also has to adjust himself to exhaust gasses from buses, trucks, and cars on a scale far beyond anything he would experience in his own city, wherever it may be. The heavy monoxide fumes added to the industrial smokes of American cities, to a person unaccustomed to them, can produce severe headaches and nausea.

There is also the matter of crowds. When Americans think of dense population masses, they are apt to think of cities in India or Japan. But nowhere in the world are more people crowded into a smaller space than in New York City. I have seen the teeming millions in Asian cities, but never have I seen greater human congestion than in the Grand Central section of New York City during the lunch hour. The business of navigating even a short distance through the crowded sidewalks calls for a special knowledge and a certain conditioning. Little wonder that people from abroad who see New York City for the first time have the feeling of being overwhelmed and exhausted—almost to the point of illness.

I have had the good fortune to be the host in the United States to visitors from Asia. And I could tell that the noonday crowds charging through New York streets produced an effect on some of them akin to panic. They had never seen so many people under such compressed conditions before. All this, combined with the new rich diet and the accelerated American pace, caused more than a few of them to long for the comparative openness of Calcutta or Tokyo.

In any event, Americans need not fear that they are in mortal jeopardy every time they leave their own country. Nor need they believe that such minor discomforts as they may encounter are the exclusive products of foreign places.

THIS DIGRESSION OUT of the way, I should like to revert to the people at Lambaréné.

Like the Schweitzer Hospital itself, the leper village was undermanned. Trudi received some assistance from the regular staff members and she had considerable assistance from the lepers themselves. But her personal workload was very heavy indeed. One of the newcomers to the Hospital, Olga Deterding, was aware of this and volunteered to work full time as her assistant. In particular, she wanted to accept responsibility for the education of the youngsters. But Olga had been at the Schweitzer Hospital only two months at the time of our visit. Her apprenticeship was not yet complete. It was necessary for her to spend a few more additional weeks on kitchen duty and mop-up detail before she would feel justified in asking Dr. Schweitzer to assign her to the leper village.

Olga Deterding came to Lambaréné almost by accident. She had started out across the African desert in a large jeep with some friends. The jeep had broken down several times and the expedition finally broke up. Olga decided to press on by herself and see something of Africa. That was how she happened to arrive at the Schweitzer Hospital. What she saw she liked and she decided to stay on and work for Dr. Schweitzer for as long as he would have her.

Olga arrived with a secret and did her best to keep it. She was the daughter of an English multimillionaire. She said nothing about her economic and social station because it might appear to others on the staff that she was staying on at Lambaréné for a lark. Also, she didn't want the staff people to feel any disparity in their relations with her.

Unfortunately for Olga there were factors beyond her control that made it impossible for her to keep her secret. Word slipped out in London, with the inevitable result that stories began to appear in the press, some of which filtered back to Lambaréné. Olga began to get cables from magazines or news services asking for permission to send writers and photographers to the Hospital to do feature stories.

All these Olga ignored. But one day Dr. Schweitzer received a cable from a Paris picture magazine saying it wanted to send staff members to the Hospital for a story built around Olga. Dr. Schweitzer, after talking to Olga, politely declined. Despite this, two days later, there arrived at the Hospital, unheralded, a French photographer-writer and his wife and a Japanese correspondent (also carrying a camera).

Olga Deterding visited Lambaréné on a safari and stayed to serve.

Olga was working in the scullery when the photographers passed.

Dr. Schweitzer was informed by the French correspondent that his editor had discovered that his magazine's files were somewhat out of date and he wanted some fresh material about the Hospital. Dr. Schweitzer was aware that the correspondents had made a long trip and did not want to send them away empty-handed. He said he would be glad to escort them around the Hospital grounds. Then he put a direct question to them: was there anything they wished?

Yes, there was. They said they would like to meet the members of the staff and do some stories about them, too.

Was there anyone in particular they would like to meet, the Doctor asked.

Why, yes; they would like to see Miss Deterding.

Well, then, said the Doctor, this was something only Miss Deterding could decide. He would put the question to her.

The reporters waited in the dining room while Dr. Schweitzer sought out Olga. Her reply was given without hesitation. She did not under any circumstances wish to see the journalists. She felt that any publicity would be inconsistent with the character of the Hospital and that of the people who worked there. She felt, too, that her purpose in staying on at Lambaréné would be defeated if she were placed in the spotlight. Besides, she was a comparative newcomer and wanted to prove herself.

Dr. Schweitzer relayed this message to the waiting reporters. They tried to convince Dr. Schweitzer that he could persuade Olga to change her mind.

The Doctor said he did not feel free to do this. Was there anything else he might do for them?

The reporters consulted among themselves and then said they were eager to accept Dr. Schweitzer's offer to escort them around the Hospital grounds.

Dr. Schweitzer replied that he would be happy to do this on condition that they would agree not to pursue Miss Deterding.

They agreed.

The tour of the Hospital began, but every now and then one of the reporters would quitely detach himself from the party and go searching for his quarry. It was apparent that they had no idea what Miss Deterding looked like, for they confronted Dr. Margaret, Albertina, Trudi, and at least three nurses and proceeded to act as though they knew the person was Olga.

They did see Olga but failed to make the identification. Olga's assignment that week happened to be kitchen detail. The reporters peered into the kitchen. It didn't occur to them that the girl with the soiled apron involved in the messy job of cleaning the innards from fish and peeling vegetables could possibly be the glamorous multimillionairess they were looking for.

It was hot in the skullery. Olga was drenched with perspiration. Her hair clung to the sides of her face. When the reporters looked at here she smiled politely. They smiled back and passed on.

Finally, the party gave up the chase and left the Hospital. When Dr. Schweitzer met us that evening in Clara's room, he sat down hard and breathed deeply.

Well, now, he said, maybe we could see the way it was. Another day very largely lost. One day is given over to filling out elaborate forms for the government. No sooner is that finished than another day has to be devoted to parrying with the fourth estate.

Then, characteristically, the Doctor's sense of humor lifted him out of his despairing mood.

"The tour of the Hospital was most thoroughly done," he said. "Even if it wasn't what they really wanted, they saw all that there was to see. Finally"—and here he grinned widely—"just to keep them occupied, I gave them a lecture on philosophy. It was a good lecture, but I'm not sure they were in a philosophical mood. Anyway, they have now gone and we can get back to our various projects."

IX

"WHICH OF YOUR two purposes do you consider more important?" Dr. Schweitzer asked. "You and Clara have said you had two principal objectives in coming here: one was concerned with my unpublished manuscripts, the other with the general question of world peace. Now, which one are you most eager to pursue?"

I told the Doctor that we felt the purposes were related, but that we were perfectly willing to have him decide which one was to be taken up first.

"But you are leaving in a few days," he said. "We may not have enough time to do both. Therefore, I ask you again: which one of your two purposes are you most bent on achieving before you leave?"

I said Clara and I had hoped to leave with some statement by him having to do with world peace. We also wanted to photograph such unpublished material as he had with him at Lambaréné. Our further presence was not essential for the statement. We had already put the case for the statement to him.

As for the manuscripts, however, this was something that would have to be done while we were at the Hospital. And since his presence was not required for the photographing of the manuscripts, Clara and I could work on this project by ourselves. We could devote the mornings to it; it shouldn't take more than three or four days.

The Doctor assented. Let us revert, however, he said, to the matter of the peace. Over the years he had been collecting materials on the question of nuclear energy, military and non-military. When he had visited Europe some months earlier, his concern had been considerably increased as a result of a meeting of Nobel Prize winners in Lindau, Germany. Many of the scientists there spoke with the utmost sense of urgency and gravity about the growing problem. Alongside the problem of peace, everything else seemed small.

Nothing to me was more striking than Dr. Schweitzer's face as he contemplated and spoke about the situation that confronted people in the world today. There seemed to be an infinity of detail in that face; it seemed as though every event in human history were clearly recorded there. Most of the time he sat forward in his straight chair, his eyes seemingly fixed on a distant object.

Only a few years ago, he added, the statement that this planet could be made unfit for life seemed absurdly melodramatic. But there was no longer any question that such power now existed. And even without a war, the atmosphere could become dangerously contaminated.

"After our earlier talk," he said, "I reflected that danger of this magnitude is not easily grasped by the human mind. As day after day passes, and as the sun continues to rise and set, the sheer regularity of nature seems to rule out such terrible thoughts. But what we seem to forget is that, yes, the sun will continue to rise and set and the moon will continue to move across the skies, but mankind can create a situation in which the sun and moon can look down upon an earth that has been stripped of all life.

"We must find some way of bringing about an increased awareness of the danger," he continued. "It is a serious thing that the governments have supplied so little information to their people on this subject. There is no reason why people should not know exactly where they stand. Every once in a while, the governments will reassure the people but this comes only after there has been a serious alarm. What is needed is genuine information. Nothing that a government knows about the nature of this new force is improper for its people to know."

Dr. Schweitzer asked me if I had brought any documentry data on the matter we were discussing.

I took out from my bag a number of papers, among them an abstract of a report, of which Dr. Willard F. Libby was a co-author, that had been prepared for the United States Atomic Energy Commission in August, 1954. The report was concerned with the effect of fallout of radioactive strontium on milk resulting from the uranium and plutonium nuclear explosions that had taken place up to that date.

Samples of milk taken from various places showed evidence of some contamination. The quantities of this radioactive strontium were found at the time to be well under dangerous levels. Even so, Dr. Libby's report showed evidence of growing apprehension, especially in his recommendation that the federal government undertake estimates on the cost of decontaminating milk. The decontamination would be effected by removing the calcium from the milk. Calcium has an affinity for radioactive strontium.

Three things were significant about that report. The first was that most of the radioactive fallout resulting from previous nuclear explosions had yet to come to earth at the time the survey was made. The second was that the biggest nuclear explosions were to occur after the report was published in August, 1954. The third was that no precise data are available on the tolerance limits of human beings to radioactive strontium.

In other forms of radiation, it is definitely known that there is far less safety than had earlier been supposed. Only ten or fifteen years ago, for example, the public was being assured that it had nothing to fear from regular X-ray examinations. More recently, however, it was disclosed that the tolerances were astoundingly lower than once had been so confidently claimed. Scientists had yet to perform the same kind of exhaustive researches into the tolerance limits of radioactive strontium that had been made on

X-ray radiation. If, through additional research, it developed that the effects of radioactive strontium had been underestimated, as in the case of X-rays, then colossal damage to all living creatures would have been done. And this is the kind of damage that cannot be undone.

The discussion with Dr. Schweitzer then turned to the power of the new bombs. One way of visualizing this new power would be to imagine a procession of one million trucks, each of which contained ten tons of TNT. The total tonnage would form a man-made mountain of dynamite several times the height of the Empire State Building. If this mountain were to be detonated it would represent the approximate power in a single twenty-megaton hydrogen bomb that can be carried by a single plane.

Dr. Schweitzer said that a very high order of public understanding throughout the world was necessary in order to deal with this problem.

I then told him that this was precisely what he was in a position to do. He was among the few individuals in the world who would have an almost universal audience for anything he might say.

His eyes turned from a distant object and he looked at me directly.

"All my life," he said, "I have carefully stayed away from making pronouncements on public matters. Groups would come to me for statements or I would be asked to sign joint letters or the press would ask for my views on certain political questions. And always I would feel forced to say no.

"It was not because I had no interest in world affairs or politics. My interest and my concerns in these things are great. It was just that I felt that my connection with the outside world should grow out of my work or thought in the fields of theology or philosophy or music. I have tried to relate myself to the problems of all humankind rather than to become involved in disputes between this or that group. I wanted to be one man speaking to another man."

I asked whether the Doctor felt that the matter we had been discussing was as much moral as it was scientific or political. I told him I believed there was no living person whose voice on such an issue would be more widely heard or respected.

Dr. Schweitzer thanked me for the compliment, but said that this was a problem for scientists. He believed that it would be too easy to attempt to discredit any non-scientist who spoke out on these matters.

I told him that I thought it inconceivable that this would be true in his case. Moreover, this was not solely a laboratory question. If nuclear power could have the effect of damaging the genes of human beings, then the nature of man himself was involved. Sovereign nations were now in a position to make decisions that were not properly theirs to make.

In saying this, I told him I recognized that the problem could not be considered apart from the larger uncertainty in the world today. Nuclear experimentation did not exist in an otherwise placid world. This, of course, added to the peril of mankind. For what we had most to fear was not merely the tests themselves, hazardous though they might be, but a saturation of tensions resulting in all-out nuclear war.

Dr. Schweitzer agreed, saying that anything that would be done against nuclear experimentation should not have the effect of putting the West at a disadvantage with respect to Soviet Russia.

He said, however, that the very real challenge of world communism should not be used as the reason for withholding vital information from the human race concerning the dangers of unlimited nuclear testing. It was possible that an informed and determined world public opinion could serve as a powerful force in bringing about enforceable agreements with respect to arms control and in leading to other long-range measures for peace.

In view of all this, I asked the Doctor whether he felt justified in putting aside his reticence about making a public statement.

He said that he would continue to give careful thought to the matter. He was still troubled, he said, about the form a constructive statement might take. How would it be issued? How would one go about drafting a statement that would be outside the context of the ideological struggle in the world today? He re-emphasized that he didn't want people to think that he was admonishing the United States or trying to intrude into domestic concerns. He wanted more time to think about these things.

When we resumed our discussion the next day he said he was still uncertain about the form of a statement or the method of its release.

Meanwhile, he was eager to consider an aspect of the problem that was highly significant. This was the fact that nations which were setting off nuclear explosions in the pursuit of their own security were possibly jeopardizing the health of other peoples.

On the basis of recent visits to Japan, I could report to Dr. Schweitzer that the Japanese government was confronted with a profound dilemma. It did not wish to oppose the American government, nor did it see any way of condemning Soviet Russia at the United Nations without including the United States. But Japan had increasing evidence of soil contamination as the result of the Russian tests and fish contamination as the result of the American tests. Autopsies had indicated the presence of radioactive strontium in a number of corpses. The American hydrogen bomb explosion called "Operation Castle" had not been under complete control. Japanese fishermen outside the prohibited area had been hit by radioactive ashes. The Japanese government had just issued instructions to its people about precautionary measures in the preparation of leafy vegetables and fish. But decontamination of food was a complicated laboratory process; it was doubtful whether even the most careful washing and boiling would be adequate.

As a result, Japanese public opinion was sensitive on the subject and was now becoming articulate and potent. Meanwhile, Communists were exploiting the issue of testing against the United States, making it appear that America was responsible for the failure to arrive at cessation agreements, and saying little about the fact of Soviet nuclear testing.

As we discussed the role of the bystanders with respect to nuclear testing, I could see that Dr. Schweitzer felt that this was a vital issue. As a citizen of a democratic nation, I did not feel that we had any right to take measures that were of possible danger to others without their consent. Indeed, the principal argument against Nazism and more recently against communism was that they were scornful of the rights of others and did harm to innocent people in their pursuit of military advantage. Is it any less immoral for any nation to jeopardize the health and safety of other peoples through uncontrolled air dispersal of radioactive poisons? If other peoples are involved, then they have a right to participate in the basic decisions involved in testing. There is no more basic tenet in democratic government than that people who are affected by the acts of government have a right to participate in the affairs of that government.

If it is wrong to impose a tax on a man without giving him a voice in government, is it any less wrong to deprive his soil or water of their purity without giving him a chance to be represented and heard?

There was no argument about any of this, the Doctor said. What concerned him was the propriety of his making any statement. It was something he wanted to think about carefully. Meanwhile, he asked me if I would put down in writing a summary of such facts on the question of nuclear fallout as I happened to have with me.

Then he got up to leave. He opened the door, then said, as though by afterthought, that he would put together the manuscript of *The Kingdom of God* and would turn it over to us in the next day or so.

X

WHEN DR. SCHWEITZER came for our meeting the next afternoon, he was carrying a small bundle. It was neatly wrapped in a large napkin. He handed it to me. "This is the manuscript of *The Kingdom of God*," he said simply. "It is practically complete."

I opened the bundle. Here, for all I knew, was one of the most important books of our time. The sheets had been perforated at the top and were tied together by a string. But I gasped when I saw the kind of paper that had been used for the manuscript. There were sheets of every size and description. Dr. Schweitzer had written his book in longhand on the reverse side of miscellaneous papers. Some of them were outdated tax forms that had been donated to Lambaréné by the French colonial administration. Some were lumber requisition forms used by a lumber mill not far away on the Ogowe River. Some came from old calendars. I couldn't even begin to count the number of manuscript pages which were written on the reverse sides of letters sent to him many years earlier.

In any other man, this would have seemed quixotic and inexplicable. In Schweitzer, however, it represented a complete consistency with everything else in his life. There was the crude piano in the dining room he wouldn't replace or repair because the money could better be used elsewhere. There was the fact that he shaved

171

without soap or lather because he considered it a luxury. There was the fact that he traveled third class only because "there was no fourth class." He could no more think of buying paper for his own literary use than he could buy an easy chair.

This, then, was *The Kingdom of God.* It was written in German longhand. The interlinear editing was prodigious. To conserve space, he had written in a very small hand. Down the right-hand margin, in even smaller longhand, were penciled notes.

Thrilled though I was with the manuscript, I was severely apprehensive over the ability of the camera to deal with such close and faded written material. I feared, in fact, that the penciled notations might be substantially lost and said so to the Doctor.

"That is nothing to worry about," he replied. "The penciled notes are for me alone. That is the way I like to write. When I sit down to my work, the first thing I do is to write my outline down the right-hand margin of each page. Then I use the main part of each sheet for the actual writing by pen."

He sat down, then bid us do likewise.

Dr. Schweitzer said that he had started the previous evening to assemble the manuscript. All the pages were in a trunk, but they had not been in the proper order. It had taken him several hours to get all the pages together and put them in sequence. I shuddered at the invasion of his time represented by this special effort.

As for *The Philosophy of Civilization,* Dr. Schweitzer feared that getting this manuscript together would take several days of uninterrupted work, at least. There were more than four hundred thousand words in the *Philosophy,* which made it several times longer than the *Kingdom.* It was doubtful, he said, that he would be able to get to this for several months. But he promised that he would make a special effort in this direction.

Then the Doctor said that if there was nothing further to discuss about the manuscript, he would like to revert to the matter of the statement about the peace.

"Even while I was sorting the manuscript papers last night and this morning I have been thinking about the declaration or state-

ment or whatever it is you want to call it," he said. "I have no
reason to believe that anything I might do or say would or should
have any substantial effect. Even so, if there would be even the
smallest usefulness that I or anyone else might have on this question, it would seem almost mandatory that the effort be made.

"This crisis intimately concerns the individual," he continued.
"The individual must therefore establish a connection with it. The
leaders of the world today have to act in an unprecedented way if
the crisis is to be met. Therefore they must be strengthened in their
determination to do the new and bold things that must be done.
That means that the individual has a greater role to play than
before. The leaders will act only as they become aware of a higher
responsibility that has behind it a wall of insistence from the people
themselves. I have no way of knowing whether I can help in this.
Perhaps I may be justified in trying."

This was the first intimation Clara and I had had that he was
giving favorable consideration to the issuing of a statement. We
exchanged glances that revealed clearly how heartened each of us
was by what the Doctor had said.

"I am still worried, however, about some of the special problems
involved in this declaration," Dr. Schweitzer resumed. "I am not
sure that I agree with you that a broad statement addressing itself
to the danger of war and the consequences of war would be the
most effective way of approaching it. Yes, the world needs a system
of enforceable law to prevent aggression and deal with the threats
to the peace, but the important thing to do is to make a start somewhere before we get into the broader questions."

He paused for a moment. Some baby goats were bleating just
outside the rear of the bungalow and he went to the screen to see
what was happening. The bleating stopped and he returned to his
seat at the end of the bed.

"I think maybe the place to take hold is with the matter of
nuclear testing," he said. "The scientific aspects of testing may be
complicated but the issues involved in testing are not. A ban on
testing requires no intricate system of enforcement. All peoples are

c.

Beach at Lambaréné: "Mankind can create a situation in which the sun and moon can look down upon an earth that has been stripped of all life."

involved, therefore the matter transcends the military interests of the testing nations. It is clearly in the human interest that the tests be stopped. Even if there is a small chance that the tests are harmful, it is important that the nations set aside the tests until they are absolutely certain what this chance involves.

"If a ban on nuclear testing can be put into effect, then perhaps the stage can be set for other and broader measures related to the peace. That is why I am inclined to a fairly limited objective. Later we will be in a better position to do the bigger things you have been talking about."

I told the Doctor that I agreed it might be easier to rally world public opinion around the need to suspend nuclear testing by all nations than it would be to deal with the basic structure of a workable peace. The main problem was war itself. But if he felt that it might be wise to confine his initial efforts to the matter of nuclear testing, I would of course respect his decision.

Dr. Schweitzer said his mind had not been finally made up on this question; he had been thinking out loud. He would continue to study the alternatives. Meanwhile, he said, there was yet another important question: what form would the statement or declaration take? How would it be issued?

Had I given any thought to these questions, he asked.

I said that I felt a direct statement, released to all the news agencies, might be effective.

He shook his head at this, saying that he had serious doubts about the news release type of story. What it gains in immediate attention it tends to lose in long-term impact. Besides, he said, one runs the risk of competing with all the other news that may be breaking on a certain day. Here he reverted to one of his favorite themes.

"I am worried about present-day journalism," he said. "The emphasis on negative happenings is much too strong. Not infrequently, news about events marking great progress is overlooked or minimized. It tends to make for a negative and discouraging atmosphere. There is a danger that people may lose faith in the forward direction of humanity if they feel that very little happens to support that faith. And real progress is related to the belief by people that it is possible.

"Well," he continued, "maybe this is the wrong time to worry how the statement is to be issued. Our first job is to bring the baby into the world. Then we can decide what to do with it We will therefore worry first about what the statement should be; then we will study it and determine how it might be used."

Mathilde Kottman came to the room and reminded us that it was getting late. I could see she was concerned about the Doctor. I stood up but the Doctor put me at my ease.

"In a way," he said, "the two of you in coming here have broken down my resolve not to involve myself in anything remotely concerned with political matters. But as I said the other day, the problem goes beyond politics. It affects all men. All men must speak. Some way must be found to bring about an increased awareness of the danger. Anything that is done should above all be simple and direct. It should not be ponderous or academic."

Once again, as he spoke, he leaned forward in an aspect of intense concentration. His eyes were closed and he seemed to measure every word. As Clara interpreted, I could see that he listened to her carefully in order to make sure that the precise nuance or emphasis would be given to what he was saying.

It was clear, both from his words and manner, that this subject was now preoccupying most of his thoughts. He looked out through the latticed window at the scudding clouds in the late afternoon sky.

"I know the weather in this part of the world like the back of my own hand," he said. "For forty-three years I have observed its habits and variations. And this is the time of the year when unfailingly there is hardly a breeze. And yet now there are winds that I have never known before. One must always be prepared, of course, for sharp changes in natural phenomena. But it is important at the same time not to ignore new factors which may not be of nature's making. Some scientific reports I have seen raise serious questions concerning the effect on weather caused by nuclear explosions. Obviously much more study is required. But at least the question exists. If there is the slightest chance that man's crops are being jeopardized, it is the duty of the nations to find out definitely before they proceed blindly."

I told the Doctor of the report *The Saturday Review* had carried by Dr. Irving Bengelsdorf of the General Electric Company in the United States. Dr. Bengelsdorf had correlated freak weather occurring in various parts of the world with hydrogen explosions and the patterns of weather movements.

"All things are now possible," Dr. Schweitzer said. "Man can hardly even recognize the devils of his own creation."

Mathilde Kottman was still waiting in the doorway. The Doctor rose to leave.

"If you are not too tired tomorrow, we can think and talk further," he said. "Meanwhile, you now have the manuscript of the *Kingdom* for such use as you wish to make of it."

Late that evening, after most of the oil lamps at the Hospital had been turned out, I walked down toward the compound. From the direction of Dr. Schweitzer's quarters I could hear the stately progression of a Bach Toccata. The Doctor was playing on the piano in his small workroom. I had heard that this piano had an organ footboard attachment so that the Doctor could keep his feet in playing condition.

I went up on the porch and stood for perhaps five minutes near the latticed window, through which I could see Dr. Schweitzer's silhouette in the dim-lighted room. Then there was a pause in the music and the Doctor called out to me. It surprised me that he should have known I was standing outside in the dark. I entered his room and he bid me sit on the piano bench next to him while he continued the Fugue. His feet moved over the organ footboard with speed and precision. His powerful hands were in total control of the piano as he met Bach's demands for complete definition of each note—each with its own weight and value, yet all of them intimately laced together to create an ordered whole.

Sitting there in the dim light with the vibrations of the Toccata racing through me, I had a stronger sense of listening to a great console than if I had been in the world's largest cathedral. I knew there might be things about Albert Schweitzer I would never comprehend or reconcile; but this particular Albert Schweitzer I felt I knew and had complete access to. The yearning for an ordered beauty; the search for a creative abandonment—yet an abandonment inside a disciplined artistry; the desire to re-create a meaningful past; the need for outpouring and release, catharsis—all these things inside Albert Schweitzer spoke in his playing. And when he was through, he sat with his hands resting lightly on the keys, his great head bent forward as though to catch any still-lingering echoes.

He was now freed of the pressures and tensions of the Hospital, with its forms to fill out in triplicate and the mounting demands of officialdom; freed of the mounds of unanswered mail on his desk; freed of the heat and the saturating moisture and the fetishers and the ants that get into the medicines. Johann Sebastian Bach had helped make it possible for Schweitzer to come to Lambaréné in the first place, through book royalties. Now Bach was restoring him to a world of creative and ordered splendor. For perhaps half an hour we chatted on that piano bench in the thin light from the flickering oil lamp at the far side of the room. He was speaking personally now—about his hopes mostly, like a young man just starting out in a career and musing about what he would like to accomplish. First, he would like to see his Hospital in tiptop running order. Second, he would like to be able to train others to run the Hospital after he is gone. Third, he would like to have just a little time to himself—to work quietly and finish his writings.

He did not wish these longings of his to give the impression that he was unhappy in his work. Actually, he never thought much about happiness or unhappiness in terms of his own life. Generally, he thought in terms of what had to be done and the time required for doing it. Now and then something would happen that would give him a sense of fulfillment and deep reward. Only a few days earlier, for example, he received word from a professorial colleague in France about an examination paper turned in by a nineteen-year-old boy. The question that had been put was: "How would you define the best hope for the culture of Western Europe?" The answer given by the student was: "It is not in any part of Europe. It is in a small African village and it can be identified with an eighty-two-year-old man."

Dr. Schweitzer paused. He held in his hand the letter that had told of the student's conception of his role in the modern world. He was profoundly moved.

"In the morning," he said, "when the sun is up and I hear the cries of the Hospital, I do not think of these lofty ideas. But at a moment like this, when the Hospital is asleep, it means much to me that the student should believe these things, whether they are true or not."

"We must find some way to bring about an increased awareness."

"There is no reason why people should not know exactly where they stand."

wanted to be one man speak-
g to another man."

ve tried to relate myself to the problems of all humankind rather than to become
ed in disputes between this or that group."

C. U.

XI

HOW DO YOU go about preparing to make copies of a literary treasure?

The problem was complicated by equatorial conditions—fungus that insisted on finding its way into the most delicate parts of precision machinery; moisture with knifelike powers of penetration; a sun directly overhead that cut down human efficiency.

Then there was the manuscript itself. From the handwritten letters of Dr. Schweitzer I had received, I thought we would probably be dealing with small, even writing in a light blue or green ink. But I wasn't prepared for the variations between pen and pencil, or the varieties of paper, some tinted and some not.

Before leaving for Lambaréné it seemed to me that, theoretically at least, the best method would be microfilming. This had to be ruled out, however, because of the size of the equipment and because there was no electricity at Lambaréné except in the operating room. While it might be possible to tap the power from the generator for our purposes, there were other problems of voltage and cycles that made this approach too complicated and risky. For the same reasons, we had to eliminate various other copying devices, some of them otherwise beautifully suited to our needs.

This left plain photography.

For two weeks before I left New York, I experimented with

various cameras borrowed from friends. I went all the way from the Italian "mini" cameras to the Speed Graphic, including my own Rolleiflex. I photographed the smallest specimens of handwriting I could find and used films with different speed ratings. Nothing I tried seemed adequate. Finally, I decided to turn the problem over to the people who knew best—Eastman Kodak of Rochester, New York. I took one of the executives, Robert Brown, into my confidence. He responded most favorably and put some of his experts on the job. Five days later, Charles Kenyon, representing Eastman Kodak, came to my office with a complete plan of battle.

First of all, he handed me a Retina IIIC. He annotated the various requirements it met:

1. Automatic unit correlating shutter speed with f.1.5 opening.
2. Built-in light meter.
3. Maximum speed and ease in reloading.
4. Handled films with 36 frames.
5. Had special magnifying attachment for close-up copying work.

Charles Kenyon said Eastman Kodak recommended that I use slow-speed Panatomic-X film. It had a fine grain and was especially adapted to enlargement problems. Then he patiently instructed me in the use of the camera, which the company would lend me.

Now, at Lambaréné, we had the manuscript of *The Kingdom of God* in our possession and it was time to get down to work.

The biggest single factor in our favor, of course, was that Clara Urquhart was a superb photographer. I had seen the high quality of her work the first time we met in New York when she showed me the proofs of her new book of photographs-with-text on Albert Schweitzer. What I had not known but now discovered was that she was an expert technician in the business of copying a manuscript.

Dr. Schweitzer had told us that he wanted the photography project to be carried out as unobtrusively as possible. He didn't want the undertaking to become a topic of conversation at the dinner table or anywhere else. Hence we could not do the work outdoors, which would have afforded the best light. We set up our improvised studio in Clara's room. We placed a low table up against the latticed window in order to have maximum light. The iron bedstand we used as the base for a clamp to which we attached the Retina IIIC. We then placed a two-inch board under the table in order to provide a camera range of fifteen inches. The close-up range finder was attached and the special lens for correct parallax was inserted. The first page of the manuscript was put into position, we crossed our fingers, drew a deep breath, and started to shoot. Clara moved with characteristic ease and dexterity as she arranged the manuscript, placing each page in position, numbering each page, and unpacking and repacking the film. All I had to do was to focus, press the trigger, and reload. By the end of the first roll, I knew that if I had been left to myself, it would have taken me two hours just to complete one spool. As it was, Clara's help enabled us to shoot thirty-six frames, or one spool, in from fifteen to twenty minutes.

On this basis, we calculated it would take about six hours to complete *The Kingdom of God*. Assuming *The Philosophy* was in the same physical condition, we guessed it would take us about eighteen hours to complete that, too. But Dr. Schweitzer was unable to put the manuscript of *The Philosophy of Civilization* together. He came to the room and said that he had gone to the trunk, looked over the manuscript, and calculated that it would take too many hours to put it together in the same orderly form in which he had given us *The Kingdom of God*. But this he would do in the months ahead; perhaps arrangements might be made for later copying.

That was entirely reasonable, I said. Meanwhile, we would at least have one of the two books on film.

As we had anticipated, the photographing of *The Kingdom* took about six hours, spread over two sessions. During the rest of the time I worked on a memorandum covering the nuclear situation as Dr. Schweitzer had requested. This memorandum was based on various documents I had brought with me to Lambaréné, including the Libby report on radioactive strontium in milk, the report of the National Academy of Science in the United States, the report of the British Academy, and the official findings of the Indian government.

The following morning at breakfast, Dr. Schweitzer told Clara that he wished to spend most of the day with us and asked if we might be available. He would come to us at 11:00 A.M. and stay with us until lunch; he would meet us again at four in the afternoon; then we would spend the evening together.

The morning meeting was devoted to a discussion of the nuclear situation. The Doctor had been giving his constant thought to it. Concerning the matter of a possible news release, of one thing he now seemed certain: a direct press statement would be unwise. It was too pretentious, smacking of publicity-seeking. Perhaps a small journal would be best. If the statement were of any value, it might be reprinted in various ways. It might stay in circulation for a period of time and have a cumulative value.

I recognized that such an approach would be entirely in character, I said. At the same time, it was important to face the likelihood that anything the Doctor said on this subject, even in a small journal, would be picked up instantly and made into headline news.

In any event, I added, it seemed clear that the best way for the Doctor to proceed would be in a manner that he felt was natural to him.

We come now to the statement itself, he said. He felt that he should not aim at any arbitrarily chosen length as being especially desirable but rather should concentrate on making the statement as clear and as complete as was humanly possible regardless of length.

"I must be careful to develop the facts very fully," he said. "I don't want to be criticized for leaving large gaps in the argument."

The Doctor then recalled an experience in Oslo in connection with the Nobel Prize. It was an experience from which he had learned a great deal.

"I was told I was expected to give an acceptance talk. I worked on the talk for several months, developing my theme with great care. When the message was completed, I estimated that it would take from seventy to eighty minutes in the reading.

"But when I arrived in Oslo I learned that I would be given thirty-five minutes for the talk. That meant cutting the message in half. I was most unhappy but I proceeded according to the limitations. The original message had been as closely knit as I knew how to make it; the shortened version was uneven and the main points inadequately developed.

"For a moment, just before I got up to speak, I was tempted to reach for the full message even at the risk of being stopped halfway through my speech. But I downed the temptation out of courtesy to my hosts. After all, it was up to them to decide what kind of program they wanted.

"The printed version, of course, was of the short talk as delivered. I didn't like it and had no interest in seeing it or acknowledging its existence. Even so, I was surprised to see how it kept being reprinted by various journals throughout the world and how long it seemed to stay alive."

He leaned back and drew a deep breath. Then he said the reason he brought up the matter was that he felt the question of length in the new statement should be put to one side; the only thing that should concern him was the accuracy and the relevance of what it was he had to say. I agreed.

What should be of most concern to him now and in the weeks ahead, he said, was to complete his study of the materials I had turned over to him. He would also correspond with some of the names I had given him and with various scientists in Europe who had expressed concern to him about these matters the last time he had seen them in Europe, at the meeting of the Nobel Laureates in Lindau, Austria.

At the afternoon meeting, he did not sit down on the edge of the bed, as was his usual manner. Instead he cleared the small table and arranged three chairs around it. He had brought with him his regular stub pen and a bottle of ink.

"We must clear up our remaining business," he said. "Are there any new matters you would like to discuss?"

I broached a subject that had been very much on my mind but that was awkward to bring up in direct discussion with him.

He said that if this had anything to do with his affairs in the event of his death, it would please him if I felt free to proceed.

What about the manuscripts? I asked. If anything should happen, who would have the authorization to edit them and approve them for possible publication?

Did I have a suggestion to make on that score, he asked.

I replied that I felt a small group, consisting perhaps of Emory Ross, J. D. Newth, his English publisher, and Clara might be in a good position to superintend the publication of the books.

"Yes, that would be a good idea," he said. "If anything happens to me, you have the authorization to bring such a group together and make the essential decisions about my unpublished work. I ask only that you observe the following conditions:

"1. That you consider carefully whether the material is actually worth publication, and, if so, what form it is to take.

"2. That nothing be added to my work of any nature.

"3. That no one be permitted to write anything in my name."

I gave him my assurance that I would convey these conditions to the other members of this literary trustee group. As I did so, however, I could not help thinking that the Doctor would probably outlive all of us. His skin had the color and texture of a man at least forty years younger. His eyes were clear and sharply focused. His hands—perhaps the most impressive hands I have ever seen on a human being, combining strength with sensitivity—were without the slightest trace of any tremor. I could recall, too, that three days earlier I had accompanied him on his "rounds," which included everything from moving large boxes of medical supplies in a hot sun and carpentry work to an inspection tour of the Hospital, walking up hill and down. He was less fatigued at the end of four hours than I was at the end of one. In fact, I found it difficult to think of any middle-aged man who could have kept up with him.

This matter disposed of, the Doctor inquired about other items of business.

I told the Doctor that a Schweitzer Fellowship group in Darien, Connecticut, was raising money for his Hospital and had asked me to obtain his autograph on various papers that might be auctioned. This commission was quickly executed.

Next, I referred to the fifteen-year-old boy, Marc Chalufour and his fight to save the old organ in his church from being replaced with a new electronic machine. Marc, who knew something about the subject, felt that the church was giving up a superior instrument, and had given me a letter for Dr. Schweitzer. The letter identified the old organ according to make and year, and reported on its condition. Marc felt that if he could have a note of support from Dr. Schweitzer, he might win over the elders.

Twenty-five years ago, as a youth myself deeply interested in the organ, I had dreamed that it might some day be possible to talk to Albert Schweitzer about the art of organ building. No man alive knew more about the Silbermann organ—the finest church organ up through the nineteenth century. And now, a letter from a fifteen-year-old boy was the open sesame. To my great delight, he spoke at length about the wonders of the Silbermann organ—about the knowledge and craftsmanship that went into it, about its tone and its unique features, about methods for keeping it in good working condition.

Then, with obvious relish, he reached for paper and pen, and wrote a letter to Master Chalufour:

Dear Marc:

If the organ was made in 1858, it is a good one. That was an age of fine organ building in Germany, France, England, and the United States. The period of good organ construction lasted from 1850 to 1885. After that, organs were built in factories. The organs built in the 1850's had an excellent tone—sweet, not too strong, but noble. If your church organ is still in reasonable good physical condition, it is certainly worth conserving and restoring, for it is most valuable.

In Alsace, there are organs dating from 1730 that are still in use in the churches; and if your church does not want the organ, perhaps you may be able to find a place for it yourself. One day its value will be realized. The old organs are better because they were built by artisans. In those days there was not the competition in price that there is today. The organ builder was able to use the finest material and did not have to count the hours necessary to put into it, as one has to do today. He could deliver an instrument of the highest quality.

Good luck from my heart to the courageous and intelligent young man who wants to save an organ.

ALBERT SCHWEITZER

The Doctor put down his pen; the conversation about the organ and the letter had taken the better part of an hour. Despite the expenditure, I had no regrets for having opened up the subject; he had enjoyed himself thoroughly.

We went off to dinner, at the end of which several members of the staff remarked that they had seldom seen the Doctor in such a joyous mood.

After dinner, Dr. Schweitzer came to Clara's room again. The first thing that had to be done, he said, was to write a letter to President Eisenhower. In this letter, he wanted to thank the President for the cordial birthday greetings. He was also eager to express his concern about the world situation, especially with reference to the armaments race. After about twenty minutes, he showed us the draft:

Lambaréné
January 10, 1957

The Hon. Dwight D. Eisenhower
The White House
Washington, D. C.

Dear Mr. President:

I send you my heartfelt thanks for your friendly letter in which you send me your good wishes and those of Mrs. Eisenhower on the occasion of my eighty-second birthday. This expression of your good

190

wishes was the first birthday greeting I received. Your generous and kind thoughts touch me deeply.

In my heart I carry the hope I may somehow be able to contribute to the peace of the world. This I know has always been your own deepest wish. We both share the conviction that humanity must find a way to control the weapons which now menace the very existence of life on earth. May it be given to us both to see the day when the world's peoples will realize that the fate of all humanity is now at stake, and that it is urgently necessary to make the bold decisions that can deal adequately with the agonizing situation in which the world now finds itself.

I was very happy to have Mr. Cousins, who will take this letter to you, here with me in Lambaréné. It was rewarding to spend time together and to see how many ideas and opinions we shared.

With assurance of my highest esteem, I am,

Yours devotedly,
ALBERT SCHWEITZER

He then wrote a final copy on thin white paper, put it into an unsealed envelope, and handed it to me to transmit to the President. He leaned back in his chair and asked whether I was glad I came to Lambaréné.

Most certainly, I replied. I hoped he didn't think it presumptuous of me if I asked him the same question.

He said he had some forty years in which to reflect on the answer to that question, so that there need be no hesitation in his reply. Yes; he was glad he came to Lambaréné, very glad. It was while he was coming up the river Ogowe one day many years ago, passing one of the luxuriant islands in the river and looking up at the scudding clouds, that the idea of reverence for life occurred to him.

Lambaréné had also made it possible for him to make his life his argument, he said.

This puzzled me and I looked up quizzically.

"As a young man, my main ambition was to be a good minister," he explained. "I completed my studies; then, after a while I started to teach. I became the principal of the seminary. All this while I had been studying and thinking about the life of Jesus and the meaning of Jesus. And the more I studied and thought, the more convinced I became that Christian theology had become over-complicated. In the early centuries after Christ, the beautiful simplicities relating to Jesus became somewhat obscured by the conflicting interpretations and the incredibly involved dogma growing out of the theological debates. For example, more than a century after Christ, there was a theological dispute growing out of questions such as these:

"Is Jesus actually God or the son of God?

"If he is God, why did he suffer? If he was the son of God, why was he made to suffer?

"What is meant by the spirit of Jesus?

"What is the true position of Mary in Christian theology?

"Elaborate theology dealing with such questions disturbed me, for it tended to lead away from the great and simple truths revealed in Jesus' own words and life. Jesus Christ did not proclaim himself to be God or the son of God; his mission was to awaken people to the Kingdom of God which he felt to be imminent.

"In my effort to get away from intricate Christian theology based on later interpretations, I developed some ideas of my own. These ideas were at variance with the ideas that had been taught me. Now, what was I to do? Was I to teach that which I myself had been taught but that I now did not believe? How could I, as the principal of a seminary, accept the responsibility for teaching young men that which I did not believe?

"But was I to teach that which I did believe? If I did so, would this not bring pain to those who had taught me?

"Faced with these two questions, I decided that I would do neither. I decided that I would leave the seminary. Instead of trying to get acceptance for my ideas, involving painful controversy, I decided I would make my life my argument. I would advocate the things I believed in terms of the life I lived and what I did. Instead of vocalizing my belief in the existence of God within each of us, I would attempt to have my life and work say what I believed."

I recalled a discussion I had had several nights earlier with Dr. Friedmann and Dr. Margaret. We agreed that it was necessary only to see Dr. Schweitzer working with his hammer or making the rounds of the Hospital to recognize a profound symbol. The symbol, of course, had to do with the carpenter and the healer.

And so I asked Dr. Schweitzer if this symbol to him was a conscious one; in short, whether he had come to Lambaréné in imitation of Christ.

When I asked the question, I couldn't be sure whether I had asked the most obvious question in the world, or whether I was pushing at a door that was meant to be kept closed.

Dr. Schweitzer looked up and said simply that the pursuit of the Christian ideal was a worthwhile aim for any man.

Then, after a moment, he said that he did not want anyone to believe what he had done was the result of hearing the voice of God or anything like that. The decision he had made was a completely rational one, consistent with everything else in his own life.

Indeed, he said, some theologians had told him that they had had direct word from God. He didn't argue. All he could say about that was that their ears were sharper than his.

He said, however, that he believed in the evolution of human spirituality, and that the higher this development in the individual, the greater his awareness of God. Therefore, if by the expression, "hearing the voice of God," one means a pure and lively and advanced development of spirituality, then the expression was correct. This is what is meant by the "dictates of the spirit."

By an advanced spiritual evolution, he emphasized that he was not thinking so much in theological terms as in ethical and moral terms. Thus he disagreed with the impression created by some of the Psalms that if people were good they would receive their reward. Goodness need not depend on rewards, or on the absence of punishments. True spiritual evolution means that there is an awareness by the individual of the natural goodness inside him; therefore he is not reaching out but actually discovering his true self when he brings the goodness to life. There is the need to do good. If one does it because he expects tangible rewards he will be mistaken.

This led to a discussion of man's expectations with respect to the Deity. If man conceived of the Deity as an omnipresent guarantor of the good he was stretching the concept of the Deity to suit his own needs and therefore he was mistaken. There is no point in expecting God to prevent injustice by man. He said that after the last great war, with all its killing and injustice, with its persecution of religious minorities and the concentration camps and gas chambers and soap made from the remains of slaughtered Jews—after all this, he did not see how it was possible to hold to the concept of a God who would intervene on the side of justice.

This, he felt, is not how God manifests himself. God manifests himself through the spiritual evolution of man and through the struggle of man to become aware of the spiritual nature of his being and then to nurture it and give it scope. The existence of evil—or the occasional triumph of the evil over the good, as in the case of persecution and concentration camps—did not mean that God was oblivious of evil or indifferent to it. It means that man had the responsibility to deal with the evil and should not sit back and expect divine intervention.

Not infrequently in history, he said, religious leaders themselves would invoke the name of God for acts that were unjust. Calvin killed his enemies; Luther failed to speak out against the persecution of Jews; the early Israelites believed at times it was their divine mission to kill; the Crusaders used the sword freely in the name of God. Modern instances were many. One example was furnished by religious Spaniards who went to Mass and then went to see creatures slaughtered in the bull ring.

To talk of the "will of God" was a presumption and often a profanation, especially when one used the term to purify ungodlike acts. Moreover, to speak of the "will of God" is to use illusion. We must accept reality. And the dominant reality, to repeat, is that God manifests himself through the human spirit. Insofar as the individual is able to discover and develop his spiritual awareness, he is at one with the Deity. Nothing is more wonderful or mysterious than the workings of the inner awareness by which man discovers his true spirituality.

I asked Dr. Schweitzer whether I detected an echo of Hegel's "only the spiritual principle, which is synonymous with God, is real." Hadn't Kant made a similar distinction—between believing God and believing *in* God?

He replied that he had always regarded Hegel as one of his most important teachers; he also reminded me of his debt to the Stoics and the early Chinese. As for Kant, he agreed with the distinction but said that so far as Kant's ideas in general were concerned, he could be impressed by them without being moved by them.

There is no reason why religion should not grow and evolve, as man himself must grow and evolve, he continued. When, for example, Apostolic belief is used as final authority for theological positions, it should be remembered that the Apostolic doctrine was not developed by the Apostles but was created by interpretation in the middle of the second century after Christ.

Theological rigidity, he feared, was hurting religion. Young people, especially, were looking to religion as a great spiritual adventure but were being disappointed because it was not searching and probing for expanding truths. Instead it was holding to fixed ideas which young people could not fully accept. There is nothing irreligious in the search for true religiosity. The more we think and the more we are aware, the greater our concentration on the development of human spirituality and the more religious we become.

A great cathedral may help to awaken the human spirit, but it cannot create it.

Each man, in a very real sense, carries his cathedral inside him.

St. Paul preached out in the open, so that all could hear. At the Hospital in Lambaréné, there is no chapel. The preaching follows the pattern of St. Paul; it is in the open.

In all these respects, the Reformation is not yet complete. It has not given adequate weight to the Christianity of the Spirit. Reformation means change; Christianity must not be afraid of change; it must not be afraid to examine and re-examine and grow. Jesus symbolized change and growth.

The ideas contained in Reverence for Life are consistent, he said, with an evolving Christianity. The door is open but Christian theology has not gone in.

To the extent that his thinking on Christian theology and religion in general have created differences of opinion, Dr. Schweitzer said that this was a matter that affected him deeply.

"I have not wished to create problems for Christianity," he said. "I have suffered deeply because some of my ideas have become problems for Christianity."

"Wasn't this what had happened to Ernest Renan?" I asked. "Didn't Renan suffer because his own thinking caused him to veer away from the tradition in which he had been brought up?"

Dr. Schweitzer replied, "It is true that Renan, who was concerned with the life and meaning of Jesus, found himself at odds with the Christian theology he himself had been taught. This caused Renan great pain. In the end it tore him to pieces because he failed to find an outlet by which he could make his own new ideas come to life. New ideas in this field of thought are powerful things. One cannot just conceive of them as mere intellectual properties and then take leave of them. My own ideas do not happen to coincide with Renan's. I am much more concerned with the actual shape of history in the life of Jesus. But I think I can understand how Renan's work affected him when he didn't allow it to redefine his life for him. This is what I mean when I say I came to Lambaréné because I wanted my life to be my argument. I didn't want my ideas to become an end in themselves. The ideas took hold of me and changed my life. Resistance to those ideas would have been impossible."

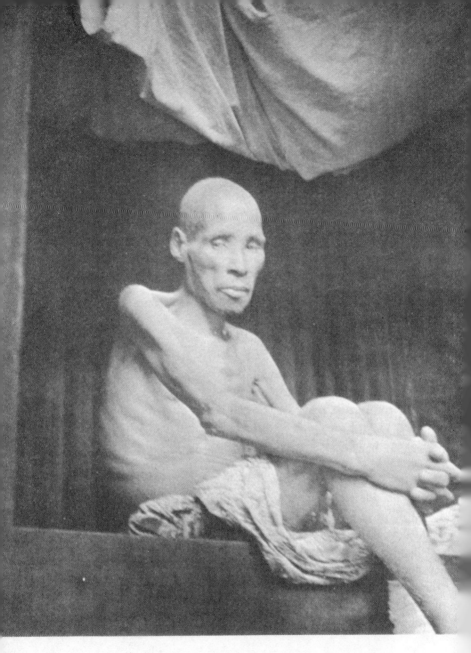

Earthquake under conscience.

Same man, same situation.

Open door.

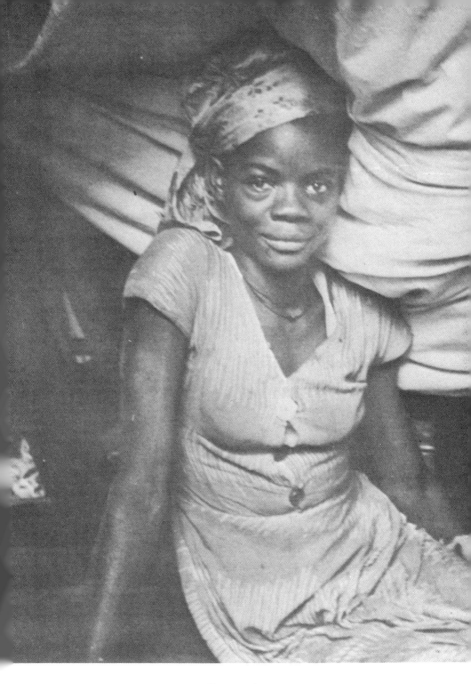

Communicator.

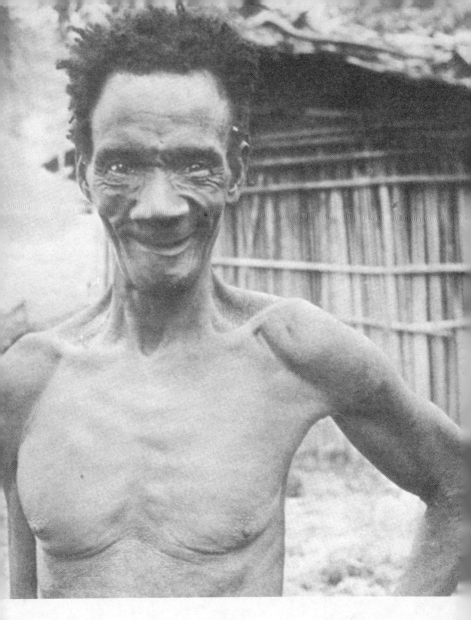

Encounter.

Special Delivery.

c.

Act One.

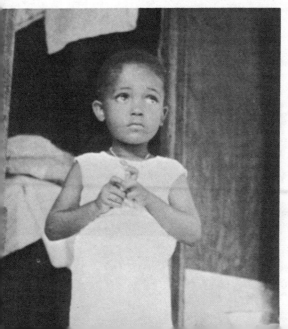

Intermission.

Responsibility as an art.

XII

THE DOCTOR GOT up to leave. It was now close to 11 P.M. I was angry with myself for having caused him to use up so much of his time, but, after his earlier admonition on this score, I had avoided any mention of the hour or the need to conserve his energies. I consoled myself with the thought that even St. Paul recognized there were limits beyond which it was unreasonable to berate a weak conscience.

I looked over at Clara. She was tranquil and content. But she had been scrutinizing me and could read my concern.

"You mustn't worry about the Doctor," she said after he left. "He does exactly what he wants to do. That is one thing no one can take from him. Besides, he feels cut off from the world and relishes the chance to talk to people from the outside.

"We should be proud and happy," she continued. "Everything we wanted to accomplish has been done. The Doctor will do the statement and it will be a good one, a very good one, and he has promised to work on his manuscripts, and I believe this time he will do it.

"You know, for the past week or so I've been watching you closely and I have the feeling that this place had no strangeness for you from the start. I don't know how to explain it except to say that you made me think you had once lived here or a place like it and knew the kind of thing to expect."

She was right about one thing: I did have a special feeling about Lambaréné long before I came. This grew not only out of Schweitzer's own descriptions of life in the jungle, but out of some experiences I had had as a child. For when I read his account of the Hospital, it made a connection with part of my boyhood.

His books had been for me, as they have been for countless others, an intense reading experience. What he wrote had the effect of reawakening incidents and ideas in one's own life. The ideas may be only half-formed in your mind, and the incidents may be part of long-slumbering memories; but they spring to life full-size under the stimulation of his descriptions. When, for example, I came across a passage in Schweitzer's *On the Edge of the Primeval Forest* I had a burst of recognition.

This particular passage was concerned with the effect of illness on Dr. Schweitzer in his early forties. His future seemed uncertain. Two operations were necessary. They were a success and the recovery was complete. After it he could write:

"The misery I have seen gives me strength, and faith in my fellow man supports my confidence in the future. I do hope I shall find a sufficient number of people who, because they themselves have been saved from physical suffering, will respond to those in need."

He had coined a striking phrase: "The Fellowship of those who bear the Mark of Pain." He identified the members of this Fellowship as "those who have learned by experience what physical pain and bodily anguish mean. They belong together, all the world over; they are united by a secret bond."

It was at this point that the magic junction of Schweitzer's ideas with my own experience took place. Years earlier, as a boy of ten, I had been sent to a public sanatorium for tuberculosis. The pain I felt was not one of sickness but of loneliness. It was the pain of being detached from everything warm and meaningful and joyous in life.

There was also the pain of being separated from hope. On Sundays I would find my perch on the wall near the entrance gate to the sanatorium and would watch the healthy people, many of them young married couples, as they walked up the hill from the bus station. They had come to visit relatives and friends but they owned the miracle of being able to leave when they wanted to. I wondered about their world of health and total option and whether they rejoiced in it. I had no reason to believe I might ever be able to join that world. The boys in my age group in the ward seldom spoke about a life beyond the sanatorium. We knew that cures took place but we also knew that although people who left the sanatorium lived a careful, disciplined life, many of them came back.

In those days, antibiotics had not yet been born and tuberculosis sanatoriums existed as much for the purpose of keeping infectious people out of society as for treating them. As a result, the outside world was something of an unreality. We longed for it but it was like pressing our noses against the windowpane of a non-existent tomorrow.

The physical suffering was not severe. There would be some dizziness, a slight fever in the evenings, but we were used to it. Most of the discomfort, I suppose, came during the winter nights. Cold was considered useful therapy at that time and the ward would be converted into open-air shelters at night. Each patient had two blankets, ample for most weather, but there were a dozen or more subzero nights during the winter when it was too cold to sleep and we shivered violently until daybreak.

There was also the pain of human relationships. As in most dependent or disciplined groups, whether in a sanatorium, school, or penitentiary, there was a sharp division between the strong and the weak. Weakness was not necessarily a biological trait but was assigned to the newcomers, who were treated as outcasts. They served the old-timers and took orders; and they marked time until the shine of their newness wore off, when they were relieved of much of their underprivileged status. It had never occurred to me until then that individuals who were in the midst of suffering themselves could be cruel, but I soon realized that when people are thrown together, whether ill or healthy, some of them assert power by being bullies, just as there are some who have positive qualities of leadership. We had our share of both, especially the former.

On occasions, there would be something of a dissolution of the animosities within the sanatorium; indeed, the dissolution would extend to the barriers that separated us from the outside world. One such occasion, of course, was at Christmas, when we put on the Nativity Play for the visitors. Even the bullies became just so many good voices in the choir. The feeling we had then of being able to join the world of the healthy and the warmth of being in their favor was a feeling I have never been able to forget. And when, years later, I sat in the section for the healthy outsiders at Trudi's leper village at the Schweitzer Hospital and watched the leper children perform in the Nativity Play, I could sense their emotions in this hour of glorious connnection with the rest of the world. I could also sense their emotions when, after many rounds of applause, the connection ceased and the outsiders returned to the universe of unlimited options. The feeling the youngsters had, I was certain, was that only a miracle would enable them to become whole again.

The miracle had happened for me at the sanatorium. Six months after being admitted, I was discharged and went back to family and school. It took many years before I could comprehend the fact that I was fully cured. I didn't quite know how to go about establishing my membership in the world of the healthy. I hesitated to ask other boys whether I could play ball with them for fear they would laugh at me. And well they might: on my fourteenth birthday I weighed seventy-eight pounds. But we lived near a public park and I invested my weekly allowance of twenty-five cents in baseball practice. I hired a boy of ten to throw grounders to me and retrieve my throws from the outfield. Within two years—some six inches taller and forty pounds heavier—I became the captain of the neighborhood baseball team, alternating between first base and shortstop. Sometimes, after league games, I would stay on the field, practicing running bases and sliding, so that I would know automatically where my feet should leave the ground without taking my eye off the ball in order to hook my slide away from the bag.

My debt to baseball was great. Even when, at college, I had a head-on collision in attempting to catch a fly ball, resulting in a serious concussion and temporary loss of memory, I almost rejoiced in the fact that this was the sort of thing that sometimes happened to healthy people in the fullest use of their physical resources. What was happening, of course, was that I was enchanted with the idea of being alive. The magic of being able to run swiftly was worth almost any price. I gloried in the fatigue and perspiration that came from muscular activity, for earlier in my life the only perspiration I had known came from fever.

Even after I was able to accept fully the fact that I could live a normal life, I carried with me the feeling that I had the obligation somehow to pay back. The sense of debt was much more than an intellectual one. It lay deep in my bones and I had no way of ignoring it. Indeed, from the moment I walked out of the sanatorium and looked back at my Sunday perch on the old wall near the entrance, I knew that my life would be unbearable unless I could find some way of making good a debt I couldn't quite define but that I knew would be with me as long as I lived.

Albert Schweitzer expressed this feeling for me in *On the Edge of the Primeval Forest* when he wrote that "he who has been delivered from pain must not think he is now free again, and at liberty to take life up as it was before, entirely forgetful of the past. He is now a man whose eyes are open with regard to pain and anguish, and he must help to overcome these two enemies and bring to others the deliverance which he has himself enjoyed."

If I felt "at home" in Lambaréné, as Clara put it, perhaps it was because there had been something in my own life years earlier that enabled me to recognize the chemistry of human emotions that existed in a place like this. I could also recognize what Schweitzer meant when he spoke about the sense of summons he felt. He was not tormented by the tragic question that has stunted the growth of civilizations—the inevitable question asked by the individual: "What can one man do?" If the purpose were strong enough, the question answered itself. The fact that thousands of doctors were required to take care of the millions of people who were in need of them in Africa did not produce in Schweitzer either awe or surrender. A single doctor, he knew, could show what was possible. In the very act of accepting a responsiblity, he could make it visible to others. Besides, to deprive one man of help because many more also needed help was to design the moral paralysis of society.

"A single doctor in Africa," Dr. Schweitzer has said, "even with the most modest equipment, can mean very much for very many. The good which he can accomplish surpasses a hundredfold what he gives of his own life and the cost of material support he must have. Just with quinine and arsenic for malaria, with novarsenobenzol for the various diseases which spread through ulcerating sores, and with emetine for dysentery, and with sufficient skill and apparatus for the most necessary operations, he can in a single year free hundreds of men from the grip of suffering and death."

It may be said that only a Schweitzer has the knowledge and personal power to answer satisfactorily the question: "What can one man do?" Certainly we can't all be Schweitzers. But what should concern us is not what it takes to be a Schweitzer but what it takes to be a man. Nature has not been equally lavish with her endowments, but each man has his own potential in terms of achievement and service. The awareness of that potential is the discovery of purpose; the fulfillment of that potential is the discovery of strength.

For Albert Schweitzer, the assertion of this potential was not a matter of charity but a matter of justice. Also moral reparations. He had always been troubled by the fact that the white man, carrying with him the cross of Jesus, not infrequently also carried the means of cheapening the lives of people he sought to change or dominate.

"Ever since the world's far-off lands were discovered, what has been the relationship of the white people to the colored?" he has asked. "What is the meaning of the simple fact that this and that people have died out, and that the condition of others is getting worse because they were 'discovered' by men who professed to be followers of Jesus? Who can measure the misery produced by the fiery liquids and hideous diseases we have brought to them?

"We are burdened with a great debt. We are not free to confer or not confer benefits on these people as we please. It is our duty. Anything we give them is not benevolence but atonement. That is the foundation from which all deliberations about 'works of mercy' must begin."

And for the appropriate time to act? The time, inevitably, is now. It can only be now. "Truth has no special time of its own." When circumstances seem least propitious, that is the correct time.

These were some of the thoughts I carried to bed with me in the bungalow overlooking the wards on my last night in Lambaréné.

XIII

The plane made a half circle as it rose from the jungle clearing. Looking out the right side I could see the fast-shrinking figure of Dr. Schweitzer slowly waving his white helmet. In a few seconds the airstrip was obscured by the jungle hills.

I observed my fellow passengers in the plane. Their faces were close to the windows. This was Lambaréné country. It had something to say to the moral imagination; its images and symbols filled the mind. I looked down at the Ogowe River and thought of the thousand-year gap between the pirogue paddled by the lepers and the man-made metal bird that had lifted us out of the jungle and into the clouds.

I thought, too, of the gap between the Hospital at Lambaréné and science in modern dress; but that was not what was important. Nor was it important that the Schweitzer Hospital should be at odds with advanced hospital design and practice. What was important was the timelessness of the Lambaréné message and the enduring nature of the teachings and the commitment and the symbol that belonged to it. The lesson was not new; in fact, it was one of the oldest lessons in the world, but it had yet to be fully understood. The lesson was concerned with the nature of human connection

Everyday is washday on the Ogowe.

One of the transportation centers at the Hospital.

and obligation, with the reality of pain, and the chemistry of human response, and the reach of the moral man.

I thought back to the long discussions I had had before coming to Lambaréné—of Clara's compassionate cautions and her concern lest I leave Lambaréné under a burden of disenchantment and hurt. I thought, too, of the talk with Frank Catchpool in the plane just before arriving at Lambaréné. And now I could dwell on these earlier cautions and anticipations in the full play of retrospect.

The biggest impression of Albert Schweitzer that emerged was of a man who had learned to use himself fully. Much of the ache and brooding unhappiness in modern life is the result of man's difficulty in using himself fully. He performs compartmentalized tasks in a compartmentalized world. He is reined in—physically, socially, spiritually. Only rarely does he have a sense of fulfilling himself through total contact with total challenge. He finds it difficult to make real connection even with those who are near to him. But there are vast yearnings inside, natural ones, demanding air and release. They have to do with his moral responses. And he has his potential, the regions of which are far broader than he can even guess at—a potential that keeps nagging at his inner self for full use. Schweitzer had never been a stranger to his potential.

This is not to say that Schweitzer achieved "happiness" in acting out that potential. He was less concerned with happiness than with purpose. What was it that had to be done? What was the best way of doing it? How did a man go about developing an awareness of important needs? How did he attach himself to those needs? Was he able to recognize the moral summons inside him? To the extent that he lived apart from these questions, he was unfulfilled and not genuinely alive.

A full life, thus defined, however, is not without the punishment of fatigue. Albert Schweitzer was supposed to be severe in his demands on the people who worked with him. Yet any demands he made on others were as nothing compared to the demands he made on himself. He was not concerned about the attainability of perfection; he *was* concerned, however, about the pursuit of perfection. He considered the desire to seek the best and work for the best as a vital part of the nature of man. When he sat down to play the piano or organ, and he was alone, he might stay with it for hours at a time. He might practice a single phrase for two hours or more. The difference between the phrase when he first played it and when he himself was satisfied with it might have been imperceptible even to a trained musical ear. But he had a stern idea of his own capacity for interpreting Bach, for example, and he felt he must stretch himself to whatever extent was necessary to achieve it. This was no mere obsession. He sought his own outermost limits as a natural part of purposeful living. If he seemed to prod and push others, it was an almost automatic carry-over of his own work habits.

There were other thoughts that occurred to me as we flew over the jungle hills of French Equatorial Africa. I considered the matter of Dr. Schweitzer's relationship with the Africans, and the many misconceptions about it that had found their way into print. When the Doctor first came to Lambaréné the life of the African had barely been touched by industrial civilization. It was difficult to get Africans to work steadily in putting up the buildings and in doing hard jobs for the Hospital.

There was the temptation at first to think that the Africans were naturally lazy. But Dr. Schweitzer very early realized that it made a difference when one lives in a climate and in an environment where the needs are few. Living close to nature, the African saw no need to work beyond that which was necessary to the immediate well-being and the minimal needs of his family. The idea of putting up extensive buildings, making concrete piles, sawing and storing woods—all this seemed to have little connection with reality as the African lived it. But the lack of incentive did not mean, as Dr. Schweitzer soon came to realize, that the Africans would not work hard under any circumstances. When they understood the reason for making a special effort, they were more than equal to the challenge.

"Watching them one day as we made an emergency trip in the canoe to save the life of a woman who was seriously ill," Dr.

Schweitzer had said, "I marveled at their stamina and their determination and I resolved never to fall into the careless habit of regarding them as shiftless."

Here we come to the real point about Schweitzer.

It is not whether he was severe in manner toward the Africans, any more than it is whether he failed to bring a gleaming modern hospital to Lambaréné.

The point about Schweitzer is that he brought the kind of spirit to Africa that the dark man hardly knew existed in the white man. Before Schweitzer, white skin meant beatings and gunpoint rule and the imposition of slavery on human flesh. If Schweitzer had done nothing else in his life than to accept the pain of these people as his own, he would have achieved eminence. And his place in history will rest on something more substantial than an argument over an unswept floor in a hospital ward in the heart of Africa. It will rest on the spotless nature of his vision and the clean sweep of his nobility.

The greatness of Schweitzer—indeed the essence of Schweitzer— is the man as symbol. It is not so much what he has done for others, but what others have done because of him and the power of his example. This is the measure of the man. What has come out of his life and thought is the kind of inspiration that can animate a generation. He has supplied a working demonstration of reverence for life. He represents enduring proof that we need not torment ourselves about the nature of human purpose. The scholar, he once wrote, must not live for science alone, nor the businessman for his business, nor the artist for his art. If affirmation for life is genuine, it will "demand from all that they should sacrifice a portion of their own lives for others."

Thus, Schweitzer's main achievement is a simple one. He has been willing to make the ultimate sacrifice for a moral principle. Like Gandhi, the power of his appeal has been in renunciation. And because he has been able to feel a supreme identification with other human beings he has exerted a greater force than millions of armed men on the march.

The Doctor and members of his staff await the arrival of a visitor.

Schweitzer to Stevenson: "That was *my* mosquito."

It is unimportant whether we call Schweitzer a great religious figure or a great moral figure or a great philosopher. It suffices that his words and works are known and that he is loved and has influence because he enables men to discover mercy in themselves. Early in his life he was accused of being an escapist. He was criticized for seeming to patronize the people he had chosen to serve. Yet the proof of his genuineness and his integrity is to be found in the response he awakens in people. He has reached countless millions who have never seen him but who have been able to identify themselves with him because of the invisible and splendid fact of his own identification with them.

"I must forgive the lies directed against myself," he wrote, "because my own life has been so many times blotted by lies. . . . I am obliged to exercise unlimited forgiveness because, if I did not, I should be untrue to myself in that I should thus act as if I were not guilty in the same way as the other has been guilty with regard to me."

Albert Schweitzer is not above criticism. Few men of our century have come closer to attaining the Greek idea of the whole man—the thinker, the leader, the man of action, the scientist, the artist. But like all great figures in history, he becomes real not despite his frailties but because of them.

Men, like history, come to life in their paradoxes. Gandhi welded a nation of four hundred million people but he couldn't hold his own family together. The cause he defined required a Congress party to fight for it, but Gandhi never gave it the power of his own name. He was the apostle of non-violence in the attainment of national freedom, but once the freedom was won he did not object to the use of military force in the Kashmir.

No man was more effective in defining and working for the liberties of the American people than Thomas Jefferson. He was permeated with the cause of human rights; he saw it in all its aspects—historically, philosophically, spiritually. His great subject in life was the anatomy of freedom. Yet he owned slaves. Like Solon and Pericles centuries before him, he made prodigious contributions to the democratic design of his nation. But, also like the Greek leaders, he did not become passionately involved in the fight against human slavery. All this is now seen in perspective. It is what Jefferson did rather than what he failed to do that inspired his generation and has given him his place in history. Moreover, the principles defined by Jefferson later became the philosophical structure for the victorious fight against slavery.

The American name most associated with the uprooting of slavery, of course, is Abraham Lincoln. Yet only a few days before he became President, Abraham Lincoln said that he did not argue against slavery where slavery existed; he would argue only against its extension to new states. He said he would not eliminate slavery in the South even if he had the power to do so. He appalled those who did not want to compromise on the issue. But when the moral summons was presented by history in its final form, Lincoln accepted magnificently.

The story of Lincoln in his relations with the Negroes would be incomplete if told only in terms of his attitudes during the early days of the Presidency. The inconsistencies and the paradoxes are neither ignored nor set aside by history; they merely yield to the consequential and to the main impact made by the man on the lives of others.

The sublimest paradox of all, of course, is represented by the fact that the most important prophecy of Jesus was proved to be historically false, yet this did not interfere with the establishment of a religion based on the total truth of his mission. Jesus prophesied the imminent end of the world. By imminent he did not mean a matter of several generations; he meant a few years. The fact that this did not eventuate was no obstacle to the creation or the growth of Christianity, based on the divinity and omniscience of Jesus. What was central and what made its impact on the spiritual nature of man were the Godlike qualities of Jesus. His example and moral teachings awakened the natural spiritual responses of people; the rest was subordinated or forgotten.

History is willing to overlook almost anything—errors, paradoxes, personal weaknesses or faults—if only a man will give enough of himself to others. The greater the ability to identify and serve, the more genuine the response. In the case of Schweitzer, later generations will not clutter their minds with petty reflections about his possible faults or inconsistencies. In his life and work will be found energy for moral imagination. This is all that will matter.

Albert Schweitzer will not be immune from attack. There may be a period of carping and intended exposure, much of it with an air of fresh discovery and all of it in a mood of disillusion. But in the long run the inconsistencies and paradoxes will be as nothing alongside the real meaning of Albert Schweitzer and his place in history. For Albert Schweitzer has done more to dramatize the reach of the moral man than anyone in contemporary Western civilization. No one in our times has taught us more about the potentiality of a human being. No one in our times has done more to liberate men of darkened skin. No one in our times has provided more inspiration.

If Albert Schweitzer is a myth, the myth is more important than the reality. For mankind needs such an image in order to exist. People need to believe that man will sacrifice for man, that he is willing to walk the wide earth in the service of man. Long after the Hospital at Lambaréné is forgotten, the symbol of Albert Schweitzer will be known and held high. It would simplify matters if Albert Schweitzer were totally without blemish, if his sense of duty toward all men carried with it an equally high sense of forbearance. But we cannot insist on the morally symmetrical. In the presence of renunciation and dedicated service such as few men are able to achieve, we can at least attempt responsible judgments and we can derive spiritual nourishment from the larger significance of his life as distinct from the fragmented reality.

There is something else we can respect: we can respect the image of Schweitzer that exists in the souls of people. This image gives them strength and purpose; it brings them closer to other people and establishes connections beyond the power of machines and explosives to alter or sever. This is what men most need for today and tomorrow but especially for today. For the making of tomorrow requires most of all a sense of connection beyond reward or compulsion. Also a sense of service that has something to do with reverence and compassion for life. This is more meaningful to man than the things he makes or the conveniences he acquires or the ornamental props of his personal kingdoms. For he reaches his full growth only as he believes in the essential beauty of the human soul. It is this that Albert Schweitzer gives him.

Albert Schweitzer is a spiritual immortal. We can be glad that this is so. Each age has need of its saints. A saint becomes a saint when he is claimed by many men as their own, when he awakens in them a desire to know the best that is in them, and the desire to soar morally.

We live at a time when people seem afraid to be themselves, when they seem to prefer a hard, shiny exterior to the genuineness of deep-felt emotion. Sophistication is prized and sentiment is dreaded. It is made to appear that one of the worst blights on a reputation is to be called a do-gooder. The literature of the day is remarkably devoid of themes on the natural goodness or even the potential goodness of man, seeing no dramatic power in the most powerful fact of the human mixture. The values of the time lean to a phony toughness, casual violence, cheap emotion; yet we are shocked when youngsters confess to having tortured and killed because they enjoyed it. Mercy and respect for life are still basic lessons in the taming of the human animal.

It matters not to Schweitzer or to history that he will be dismissed by some as a do-gooder or as a sentimentalist who frittered his life away on Africans who couldn't read or write. "Anyone who proposes to do good," he wrote, "must not expect people to roll stones out of his way, but must accept his lot calmly if they even roll a few more upon it." For the tragedy of life is not in the hurt to a man's name or even in the fact of death itself. The tragedy of life is in what dies inside a man while he lives—the death of genuine feeling, the death of inspired response, the death of the awareness that makes it possible to feel the pain or the glory of other men in oneself.

Schweitzer's aim was not to dazzle an age but to awaken it, to make it comprehend that moral splendor is part of the gift of life, and that each man has unlimited strength to feel human oneness and to act upon it. He has proved that although a man may have no jurisdiction over the fact of his existence, he can hold supreme command over the meaning of existence for him. Thus, no man need fear death; he need fear only that he may die without having known his greatest power—the power of his free will to give his life for others.

If there is a need in America today, it is for Schweitzers among us. We are swollen with meaningless satisfactions and dulled by petty immediacies—but the threat to this nation and its freedoms and to human life in general has never been greater. To the extent that part of this threat is recognized, it is assumed it can be adequately met by a posture of military and material strength. But the crisis is basically moral and demands moral strength.

We can't save the nation by acting as though only the nation is in jeopardy, nor by acting as though the highest value is the nation. The highest value is the human being and the human potential. In order to safeguard this human potential we have to do more than to surround ourselves with high explosives. We have to make the supreme identification with other people, including those who are different from us or who have less than we. If sacrifice is required, we shall have to sacrifice. If we are to lead, what we say and what we do must become more important in our own minds than what we sell or what we use. At a time when men possess the means for demolishing a planet the only business that makes sense is the business of inspired purpose.

We live in eternal dread of hunger; but we shall never escape the hunger inside us if we are starved for inspiration or are empty of vital purpose. And if we see not at all into these things, the things that make for a single body of all those who now live or who have ever lived, then we shall have lived only half a life. It is in this sense that Albert Schweitzer has helped to make men whole.

We can rejoice in this, for Schweitzer has given an infusion of spiritual energy to our age that is real and that will persist.

Returning home, I felt happy that my two specific purposes in going to Lambaréné had been met. But even more important was the fact that the image of Albert Schweitzer I carried away with me was intact—fortified, if anything, by a direct view. For at Lambaréné I learned that a man does not have to be an angel to be a saint.

Horizon time.

APPENDIX

The first part of Albert Schweitzer's statement, "Peace or Atomic War?" was completed in Lambaréné early in April 1957. It was released to the world by Radio Oslo on April 24, 1957. Four years earlier, Dr. Schweitzer had gone to Oslo to accept the Nobel Peace Prize, the money from which went into the building of the leper hospital at Lambaréné.

Again, in April 1958, Radio Oslo issued a second Schweitzer declaration for world broadcast and publication.

The text of the complete statement appears on the following pages.

Peace or Atomic War?

by *Albert Schweitzer*

PART I

SINCE MARCH 1, 1954, hydrogen bombs have been tested by the United States at the Pacific island of Bikini in the Marshall group and by Soviet Russia in Siberia. We know that testing of atomic weapons is something quite different from testing of non-atomic ones. Earlier, when a new type of giant gun had been tested, the matter ended with the detonation. That is not the case after the explosion of a hydrogen bomb. Something remains in the air, namely, an incalculable number of radioactive particles emitting radioactive rays. This was also true of the uranium bombs dropped on Nagasaki and Hiroshima and those which were subsequently tested. However, not much attention was given to this fact because these bombs were smaller and less effective than the hydrogen bombs.

Since radioactive rays of sufficient amount and strength have harmful effects on the human body, it must be considered whether the radiation resulting from the hydrogen explosions that have already taken place represents a danger which would increase with new explosions.

In the course of the three-and-a-half years that have passed since then [the test explosions of the early hydrogen bombs] representatives of the physical and medical sciences have been studying the problem. Observations on the distribution, origin, and nature of radiation have

227

been made. The processes through which the human body is harmfully affected have been analyzed. The material collected, although far from complete, allows us to draw the conclusion that radiation resulting from the explosions which have already taken place represents a danger to the human race—a danger not to be underrated—and that further explosions of atomic bombs will increase this danger to an alarming extent.

Although this conclusion has repeatedly been expressed, especially during the last few months, it has not, strange to say, influenced public opinion to the extent that one might have expected. Individuals and peoples have not been aroused to give to this danger the attention it unfortunately deserves. It must be demonstrated and made clear to them.

I raise my voice, together with those of others who have lately felt it their duty to act, through speaking and writing, in warning of the danger. My age and the generous understanding so many people have shown of my work permit me to hope that my appeal may contribute to preparing the way for the insights so urgently needed.

My thanks go to the radio station in Oslo, the city of the Nobel Peace Prize, for making it possible for what I feel I have to say to reach far-off places.

What is radioactivity?

Radioactivity consists of rays differing from those of light in being invisible and able to pass not only through glass but also through thin metal discs and layers of cell tissue in the human and animal bodies. Rays of this kind were first discovered in 1895 by the physicist Wilhelm Roentgen of Munich, and named after him.

In 1896 the French physicist Henri Becquerel demonstrated that rays of this kind occur in nature. They are emitted from uranium, an element known since 1786.

In 1898 Pierre Curie and his wife discovered in the mineral pitch-blende, a uranium ore, the strongly radioactive element radium.

The joy that such rays were at the disposal of humanity was at first unmixed. For the rays appeared to influence the relatively fast growing and decaying cells of malignant tumors and sarcomas. If exposed to these rays repeatedly for a longer period, some of the terrible neoplasms could be destroyed.

After a time it was found, however, that the destruction of cancer cells does not always mean the cure of cancer, and that the normal cells of the body may be seriously damaged if long exposed to radioactivity.

When Mme. Curie, after handling uranium ore for four years, finally held the first gram of radium in her hand, there appeared abrasions in the skin which no treatment could cure. With the years she grew steadily sicker from a disease caused by radioactive rays which damaged her bone marrow and through this her blood. In 1934 death ended her suffering.

Even so, for many years we were not aware of the grave risks involved in X-rays to those constantly exposed to them. Through operating X-ray apparatus thousands of doctors and nurses have incurred incurable diseases.

Radioactive rays are material things. Through them the radioactive element constantly and forcefully emits tiny particles of itself. These are of three kinds, named after the three first letters of the Greek alphabet: *alpha, beta, gamma.* The gamma rays are the hardest and have the strongest effect.

The reason why elements emit radioactive rays is that they are constantly decaying, and radioactivity is the energy they liberate little by little. There are other elements besides uranium and radium which are radioactive. To the radiation from the elements in the earth is added some radiation from space. Fortunately, the air mass 250 miles high that surrounds our earth protects us against this radiation. Only a very small fraction of it reaches us.

We are, then, constantly being exposed to radioactive radiation coming from the earth and from space. It is so weak, however, that it does not hurt us. Stronger sources of radiation, as for instance X-ray machines and exposed radium, have, as we know, harmful effects if one is exposed to them for some time.

Radioactive rays are, as I said, invisible. How can we tell that they are there and how strong they are?

Thanks to the German physicist Hans Geiger, who died in 1945 as a victim to X-rays, we have an instrument which makes that possible. This instrument, called the Geiger counter, consists of a metal tube containing rarefied air. In it are two metal electrodes between which there is a high potential. Radioactive rays from the outside affect the tube and release a discharge between the two electrodes. The stronger the radiation, the quicker the discharges follow one another. A small device connected to the tube makes the discharge audible. The Geiger counter performs a veritable drum-roll when the discharges are strong.

There are two kinds of atom bomb—uranium bombs and hydrogen bombs. The effect of a uranium bomb is due to a process which liberates energy through the fission of uranium. In the hydrogen bomb the liberation of energy is the result of the transformation of hydrogen into helium.

It is interesting to note that this latter process is similar to that which takes place in the center of the sun, supplying it with the self-renewing energy which it emits in the form of light and heat.

In principle, the effect of both bombs is the same. But according to various estimates the effect of one of the latest hydrogen bombs is 2,000 times stronger than the one dropped on Hiroshima.

To these two bombs has recently been added the cobalt bomb, a kind of super atom bomb. It is a hydrogen bomb surrounded by a layer of cobalt. Its effect is estimated to be many times stronger than that of any hydrogen bomb made so far.

The explosion of an atom bomb creates an inconceivably large number of exceedingly small particles of radioactive elements which decay like uranium or radium. Some of these particles decay very quickly, others more slowly, and some with extraordinary slowness. The strongest of these elements cease to exist only ten seconds after the detonation of the bomb. But in this short time they may have killed a great number of people in a circumference of several miles.

What remains are the less powerful elements. In our time it is with these we have to contend. It is of the danger arising from the radioactive rays emitted by these elements that we must be aware.

Of these elements some exist for hours, some for weeks, months, years, or even millions of years, undergoing continuous decay. They float in the higher strata of air as clouds of radioactive dust. The heavy particles fall down first. The lighter ones will stay in the air for a longer time or come down with rain or snow. How long it will take until everything carried up in the air by past explosions has disappeared no one can say with certainty. According to some estimates, this will not happen sooner than thirty or forty years from now.

As a boy I witnessed how dust hurled into the air from the explosion in 1883 of the island Krakatoa in the Sunda group was so noticeable for two years afterwards that sunsets were given extraordinary splendor by it.

What we can state with certainty, however, is that the radioactive clouds will constantly be carried by the winds around the globe and that some of the dust, by its own weight, or by being brought down little by little, by rain, snow, mist, and dew, will fall down on the hard surface of the earth, and into rivers and oceans.

Of what nature are these radioactive elements, particles of which, carried up in the air by the explosion of atom bombs, are now falling down again?

They are strange variants of the usual non-radioactive elements, having the same chemical properties, but a different atomic weight. Their names are always accompanied by their atomic weights. The same element can occur in several radioactive variants. Besides Iodine 131, which lasts for only sixteen days, we have Iodine 129, which lasts for 200,000,000 years.

Dangerous elements of this kind are Phosphorus 32, Calcium 45, Iodine 131, Iron 55, Bismuth 210, Plutonium 239, Cerium 144, Strontium 89, Caesium 137. If the hydrogen bomb is covered with cobalt, Cobalt 60 must be added to the list.

Particularly dangerous are the elements combining long life with a relatively strong, efficient radiation. Among them Strontium 90 takes the first place. It is present in very large amounts in radioactive dust. Cobalt 60 must also be mentioned as particularly dangerous.

The radioactivity in the air, increased through these elements, will not harm us from the outside, not being strong enough to penetrate the skin. It is another matter with respiration, through which radioactive elements can enter our bodies. But the danger which has to be stressed above all the others is the one which arises from our drinking radioactive water and eating radioactive food as a consequence of the increased radioactivity in the air.

Since the explosions of Bikini and Siberia, rain falling over Japan has, from time to time, been so radioactive that the water from it cannot be drunk. Not only that: reports of radioactive rainfall are coming from all parts of the world where analyses have recently been made. In several places the water has proved to be so radioactive that it was unfit for drinking.

Well-water becomes radioactive to any considerable extent only after longer periods of heavy rainfall.

Wherever radioactive rainwater is found, the soil is also radioactive —and in a higher degree. The soil is made radioactive not only by the downpour, but also from radioactive dust falling on it. And with the soil the vegetation will also have become radioactive, because radioactive elements deposited in the soil pass into the plants, where they are stored. This is of importance, for as a result of this process we may be threatened by a considerable amount of radioactive elements. Radioactive elements in grass, when eaten by animals whose meat is used for food, will be absorbed and stored in our bodies. Or we may absorb them by drinking milk from cows grazing on contaminated soil. In that way small children run an especially dangerous risk of absorbing radioactive elements. When we eat contaminated cheese and fruits the radioactive elements stored in them are transferred to us.

What this storing of radioactive material implies is clearly demonstrated by the observations made when the radioactivity of the Columbia River in North America was analyzed. The radioactivity was caused by the atomic plants at Hanford, which produce plutonium for atomic bombs and which empty their waste water into the river. The radioactivity of the river water was insignificant. But the radioactivity of the river plankton was 2,000 times higher, that of the ducks eating plankton 40,000 times higher, that of the fish 15,000 times higher. In young swallows fed on insects caught by their parents in the river the radioactivity was 500,000 times higher, and in the egg yolks of water birds more than 1,000,000 times higher.

From official and unofficial sources we have been assured, time and time again, that the increase in radioactivity of the air does not exceed the amount the human body can tolerate without any harmful effects. This is just evading the issue. Even if we are not directly affected by the radioactive material in the air, we are indirectly affected through that which has fallen down, is falling down, and will fall down. We are absorbing this through radioactive drinking water and through animal and vegetable foodstuffs, to the same extent as radioactive elements are stored in the vegetation of the region in which we live. Unfortunately for us, nature hoards what is falling down from the air.

None of the radioactivity of the air created by the explosion of atom bombs is so unimportant that it may not, in the long run, become a danger to us through increasing the amount of radioactivity stored in our bodies.

What we absorb of radioactivity is not spread evenly in all cellular tissue. It is deposited in certain parts of our body, particularly in the bone tissue and also in the spleen and in the liver. From those sources the organs which are especially sensitive to it are exposed to radiation. What the radiation lacks in strength is compensated for by time. It works day and night without interruption.

How does radiation affect the cells of an organ? Through being ionized, that is to say, electrically charged. This change means that the chemical processes which make it possible for the cells to do their job in our body no longer function as they should. They are no longer able to perform the tasks which are of vital importance to us. We must also bear in mind that a great number of the cells of an organ may degenerate or die as a result of radiation.

What are the diseases caused by internal radiation? The same diseases that are known to be caused by external radiation.

They are mainly serious blood diseases. The cells of the red bone marrow, where the red and the white blood corpuscles are formed, are very sensitive to radioactive rays. It is these corpuscles, found in great numbers in the blood, which make it possible for it to play such an important part. If the cells in the bone marrow are damaged by radiation they will produce too few or abnormal, degenerating blood corpuscles. Both cases lead to blood diseases and, frequently, to death. These were the diseases that killed the victims of X-rays and radium rays.

It was one of these diseases that attacked the Japanese fishermen who were surprised in their vessel by radioactive ashes falling down 240 miles from Bikini after the explosion of a hydrogen bomb. Being strong and only mildly affected, all but one were saved by continued blood transfusions.

In the cases cited the radiation came from the outside. It is unfortunately very probable that internal radiation affecting the bone marrow and lasting for years will have the same effect, particularly since the radiation goes from the bone tissue to the bone marrow. As I have said, the radioactive elements tend to be stored in the bone tissue.

Internal radiation threatens not only our own health but also that of our descendants. The cells of the reproductive organs are particularly vulnerable to radiation, which attacks the nucleus to such an extent that it can be seen in the microscope. Profound damage to these cells results in corresponding damage to our descendants, such as stillbirths and the births of babies with mental or physical defects.

In this context also, we can point to the effects of radiation coming from the outside. It is a fact—even if the statistical material being published in the press needs checking—that in Nagasaki, during the years following the dropping of the atom bomb, an exceptionally high occurrence of stillbirths and of deformed children was observed.

In order to establish the effect of radioactive radiation on posterity, comparative studies have been made between the descendants of doctors who have been using X-ray apparatus over a period of years and descendants of doctors who have not. The material of this study comprises about 3,000 doctors in each group. A noticeable difference was found. The descendants of radiologists showed a percentage of stillbirths of 14.03, while the percentage among the non-radiologists was 12.22. In the first group 6.01 per cent of the children had congenital defects, while only 4.82 per cent in the second. The number of healthy children in the first group was 80.42 per cent; in the other it was significantly higher, viz. 83.23 per cent.

It must be remembered that even the weakest of internal radiation can have harmful effects on our descendants. The total effect of the damage done to descendants of ancestors who have been exposed to radioactive rays will not, in accordance with the laws of genetics, be apparent in the generations coming immediately after us. The full effects will appear only 100 or 200 years later.

As the matter stands we cannot at present cite cases of serious damage done by internal radiation. To the extent that such radiation exists it is not sufficiently strong and has not lasted long enough to have caused the damage in question. We can only conclude from the harmful effects known to be caused by external radiation what we must expect in the future from internal radiation.

If the effect of the latter is not as strong as that of the former, it may become so through working little by little and without interruption. The final result will be the same in both cases. Their effects add up.

We must also remember that internal radiation, unlike that from outside, does not have to penetrate layers of skin, tissues, and muscles to hit the organs. It works at close range and without any weakening of its force.

When we realize under what conditions internal radiation is working, we cease to underrate it. Even if it is true that, when speaking of the dangers of internal radiation, we can point to no actual case and only express our fear, that fear is so solidly founded on facts that it attains the weight of reality in determining our attitude. We are forced to regard every increase in the existing danger through further creation of radioactive elements by atom bomb explosions as a catastrophe for the human race, a catastrophe that must be prevented.

There can be no question of doing anything else, if only for the reason that we cannot take the responsibility for the consequences it might have for our descendants. They are threatened by the greatest and most terrible danger.

That radioactive elements created by us are found in nature is an astounding event in the history of the earth and of the human race. To fail to consider its importance and its consequences would be a folly for which humanity would have to pay a terrible price. We are committing a folly in thoughtlessness. We must not fail to pull ourselves together before it is too late. We must muster the insight, the seriousness, and the courage to leave folly and to face reality.

This is at bottom what the statesmen of the nations producing atomic bombs are thinking, too. Through the reports they are receiving they are sufficiently informed to arrive at their own judgments, and we must also assume that they are alive to their responsibility.

At any rate, America and Soviet Russia and Britain are telling one another again and again that they want nothing more than to reach an agreement to end the testing of atomic weapons. At the same time, however, they declare that they cannot stop the tests so long as there is no such agreement.

Why do they not come to an agreement? The real reason is that in their own countries there is no public opinion asking for it. Nor is there any such public opinion in other countries, with the exception of Japan. This opinion has been forced upon the Japanese people because, little by little, they will be hit in a most terrible way by the evil consequences of all the tests.

An agreement of this kind presupposes reliability and trust. There must be guarantees preventing the agreement from being signed by anyone intending to win important tactical advantages foreseen only by him. Public opinion in all nations concerned must inspire and accept the agreement.

When public opinion has been created in the countries concerned and among all nations, an opinion informed of the dangers involved in going on with the tests and led by the reason which this information imposes, then the statesmen may reach an agreement to stop the experiments.

A public opinion of this kind stands in no need of plebiscites or committees to express itself. It works through just being there.

The end of further experiments with atom bombs would be like the early sunrays of hope which suffering humanity is longing for.

Part II

IN APRIL of last year I, together with others, raised my voice to draw attention to the great danger of radioactive poisoning of the air and the earth, following tests with atomic and hydrogen bombs. With others, I appealed to the nuclear powers to come to a workable agreement to stop the tests as soon as possible and declare their genuine desire to renounce the use of nuclear weapons.

At that time there appeared to be reasonable hope that this step would be taken. It was not. The negotiations in London last summer achieved nothing. The conference arranged by the United Nations in the autumn of last year suffered the same fate when the Soviet Union withdrew from the discussions.

The question of nuclear arms control, however, cannot be put aside. Any discussions among the major nations will have to consider this problem.

Cessation of nuclear tests has often been proposed as the first step in any comprehensive and workable plan for arms control.

One might have thought it would be comparatively simple for all those involved to agree on this first step. No nuclear power would have to sacrifice any of the atomic weapons in its possession. The disadvantage of not being able to try out new bombs or nuclear devices would be the same for all.

237

The United States and Great Britain have been reluctant to take the first step. They spoke against it when the matter was discussed in the spring of 1957. Since then many statements have been issued claiming that radioactivity resulting from nuclear tests is not dangerous. For example, in an official statement coming from the United States, we read the following: "The necessary steps should be taken to correct the present confusion of the general public [with respect to the effects of testing]. . . . The present and potential effects on heredity from the gradual increase of radioactivity in the air are kept within tolerable limits. . . . The possibility of harmful effects which people believe to be outside control has a strong emotional impact. . . . The continuation of nuclear tests is necessary and justified in the interests of national security."

Despite these assurances, however, people are becoming increasingly apprehensive concerning the possible dangers resulting from nuclear tests.

The reasoning behind the somewhat obscure statement that "the effects on heredity from the gradual increase of radioactivity in the air are kept within tolerable limits" is that the number of deformed children that will be born as a result of the harm done to the sexual cells supposedly will not be large enough to justify stopping the tests.

During this campaign of reassurance, a prominent American nuclear physicist even declared that the luminous watchdials in the world represent a greater danger than the radioactive fall-out of nuclear tests thus far.

This campaign of reassurance sets up anticipations of glad tidings that science has succeeded in making the prototype of a hydrogen bomb with a considerably less dangerous radioactive fall-out. The new explosive is called a "clean" hydrogen bomb. The old type is being designated as the "dirty" bomb.

The so-called "clean" hydrogen bomb differs from the other in having a jacket made of a material which does not release immense quantities of radioactive elements at the enormous explosion temperature. That is why it is less harmful, as regards radioactivity, than the usual ones.

However, the new highly praised hydrogen bomb is—let it be said in passing—only relatively clean. Its trigger is a uranium bomb made of the fissionable Uranium-235—an atomic bomb as powerful as the one dropped over Hiroshima. This bomb, when detonated, also produces radioactivity, as do the neutrons released in great numbers at the explosion.

Earlier this year, in an American newspaper, Edward Teller, the father of the "dirty" hydrogen bomb, sings a hymn of praise to the idyllic nuclear war to be waged with completely clean hydrogen bombs. He insists on a continuation of the tests in order to perfect this ideal bomb.

Here are two stanzas from Edward Teller's hymn to idyllic nuclear warfare:

"Further tests will put us into a position to fight our opponents' war machine, while sparing the innocent bystanders."

"Clean weapons of this kind will reduce unnecessary casualties in a future war."

The idea of limited nuclear war is a contradiction in terms. Each side will use all the power at its disposal in an attempt to annihilate the enemy. The U.S. Department of Defense has quite recently declared that the irradiation of whole areas has become a new offensive weapon.

The "clean" hydrogen bomb may be intended, I fear, more for display-case purposes than for use. The intention seems to be to convince people that new nuclear tests will be followed by less and less radiation and that there is no real argument for the discontinuation of the tests.

Those who think that the danger created by nuclear tests is small mainly take the air radiation into consideration, and persuade themselves to believe that the danger limit has not yet been reached.

The results of their arithmetic are not so reliable, however, as they would have us believe. Through the years the toleration limit for radiation has had to be lowered several times. In 1934 it was 100 radiation units per year. At present the limit is officially put at 5. In many countries it is even lower. Dr. Lauriston Taylor (U.S.A.), who is regarded as an authority on protection against radiation, holds—like others—that it is an open question whether there is such a thing as a harmless amount of radiation. He thinks that we can speak only of an amount of radiation which we regard as tolerable.

We are constantly being told about a "maximum permissible

amount" of radiation. What does "permissible" mean? And who has the right to "permit" people to be exposed to these dangers?

When speaking about the risk of radiation we must consider not only the radiation coming from the outside, but also the radioactivity that gets into our bodies.

What is the source of this radioactivity?

The radioactive materials put into the air by nuclear tests do not stay there permanently. In the form of radioactive rain—or even radioactive snow—they fall to the earth. They enter the plants through leaves and roots and stay there. We absorb them by drinking milk from cows or by eating the meat of animals which have fed on it. Radioactive rain contaminates our drinking water.

The most powerful radioactive poisoning occurs in the areas between the Northern latitudes 10° and 60°, because of the numerous nuclear tests conducted mainly in these latitudes by the Soviet Union and the United States.

The radioactive elements absorbed over the years by the body are not evenly distributed in the cellular tissue, but deposited and accumulated at certain points. From these points internal radiation takes place, causing injuries to particularly vulnerable organs. What this kind of radiation lacks in strength is made up for by its longevity, working as it does for years, day and night.

It is a well-known fact that one of the most widespread and dangerous elements absorbed by us is Strontium 90. It is stored in the bones and from there emits its rays into cells of red bone marrow, where the red and white corpuscles are made. If the radiation is too great, blood diseases—fatal in most cases—are the result.

The cells of the reproductive organs are particularly sensitive. Even relatively weak radiation may lead to fatal consequences.

The most sinister aspect of internal as well as external radiation is that years may pass before the evil consequences appear. Indeed, they make themselves felt, not in the first or second generation, but in those that follow. Generation after generation, for centuries to come, will witness the birth of an ever-increasing number of children with mental and physical defects.

It is not for the physicist, choosing to take into account only the radiation from the air, to utter the final word on the dangers of nuclear tests. That right belongs to the biologists and physicians who have studied internal as well as external radiation, and to those scientists who pay attention to the facts established by the biologists and physicians.

The declaration signed by 9,235 scientists of all nations, handed to the Secretary General of the U.N. by Dr. Linus Pauling on January 13, 1958, gave the campaign of reassurance a serious blow. The scientists declared that the radioactivity gradually created by nuclear tests represents a grave danger for all parts of the world, particularly serious because its consequences will be an increasing number of deformed children in the future. For this reason they insist on an international agreement putting an end to the nuclear tests.

The declaration signed by the 9,235 scientists did well in stressing the danger of the harmful effects of nuclear tests on future generations resulting, according to biologists and physicians, from the radiation to which we are now being exposed.

We must not disregard our responsibility to guard against the possibility that thousands of childen may be born with the most serious mental and physical defects. It will be no excuse for us to say later that we were unaware of that possibility. Only those who have never been present at the birth of a deformed baby, never witnessed the whimpering cries of its mother, should dare to maintain that the risk of nuclear testing is small. The well-known French biologist and geneticist Jean Rostand calls the continuation of nuclear tests "a crime into the future" (*le crime dans l'avenir*). It is the particular duty of women to prevent this sin against the future. It is for them to raise their voices against it in such a way that they will be heard.

No longer can we take any comfort from the fact that the scientists do not agree on the danger of radiation, nor that we must await the decision of international bodies before making positive statements about radiation. Despite all the claims of safety, the truth about the danger of nuclear explosions marches imperturbably along, influencing an ever-increasing section of public opinion. In the long run, even the most well-organized propaganda can do nothing against the truth.

It is a strange fact that few people have taken into consideration that the question of nuclear testing is not one which concerns the nuclear powers exclusively, a question for them to decide at their pleasure. Who has given these countries the right to experiment, in times of peace, with weapons involving the most serious risks for the whole world? What has international law—enthroned by the United Nations and so highly praised in our time—to say on this matter? Does it no longer look out on the world from its temple? Then let it go out, so that it may face the facts and do its duty accordingly.

International law should consider at once the compelling case of Japan. That country has suffered heavily from the effects of nuclear tests. The radioactive clouds created by the Soviet tests in Northeast Siberia and by the American tests in the Pacific Ocean are carried by the winds over Japan. The resultant radioactive poisoning is considerable. Powerful radioactive rainfalls are quite common. The radioactive poisoning of the soil and the vegetation is so heavy that the inhabitants of some districts ought to abstain from using their harvest for food. People are eating rice contaminated by radioactive strontium, a substance particularly dangerous for children. The ocean surrounding Japan is also at times dangerously radioactive, and thereby the very food supply of the country—in which fish has always played an important part—is being threatened.

As every new nuclear test makes a bad situation worse, the Japanese ministers, having heard of plans for new tests to the north or south of Japan, have presented their country's urgent appeal in Washington or Moscow, beseeching the American or Soviet authorities to give up their plans.

We generally learn about these appeals and the refusals through short newspaper items. Unfortunately, there have been few responsible editorials drawing our attention to the stories behind the news—the misery of human beings who are now in jeopardy. In that respect we and the press are guilty of a lack of compassion. Even guiltier, however, is international law, which has kept silent and indifferent on this question, year after year.

It is high time to recognize that the question of nuclear testing is a matter for world law to consider. Mankind is imperiled by the tests. Mankind insists that they stop, and has every right to do so.

If anything is left of international law in our civilization, then the nations responsible for nuclear tests must renounce them immediately, without making this renunciation dependent on agreements concerning the larger questions of general disarmament. Nuclear tests have nothing to do with disarmament. The nations in question will continue to have the weapons they now have.

There is no time to lose. New tests must not be allowed to increase the already existing danger. It is important to realize that even without new tests the danger will increase during the coming years: a large part of the radioactive elements flung up in the atmosphere and stratosphere at the nuclear experiment is still there. It will come down only after several years—probably about fifteen.

The immediate renunciation of further tests will create a favorable atmosphere for talk on controlling the stockpiles of nuclear weapons and banning their use. When this urgently necessary step has been taken, such negotiations can take place in peace.

That the Soviet Union has announced its willingness to stop its tests is of great importance. The world now looks to the United States and Great Britain for the kind of moral initiative and action that goes along with great leadership.

*　　*　　*

Today we are faced with the menacing possibility of an outbreak of atomic war between Soviet Russia and the United States. It can only be averted if the two powers decide to renounce atomic arms.

How did this situation arise?

In 1945 America succeeded in producing an atomic bomb with Uranium 235. On August 6, 1945, this bomb was dropped on Hiroshima. Another atomic bomb was dropped on Nagasaki on August 9.

When America came into the possession of such a bomb it held a military advantage over other countries.

In July 1949 the Soviet Union also test-exploded its first nuclear bomb. Its power was approximately equal to the American bomb then existing.

On October 3, 1952, England exploded its first atomic bomb on the Isle of Montebello (situated on the northwest coast of Australia).

In the quest for nuclear supremacy, both the Soviet Union and the United States moved toward the development of a nuclear weapon many times more powerful—the hydrogen bomb. A series of tests was undertaken by the United States in the Marshall Islands beginning in May, 1951, and culminating in a successfully exploded hydrogen bomb in March 1954.

The actual power of the explosion was far stronger than had been originally calculated.

At approximately the same time, the Soviet Union also started its experimentations, exploding its first hydrogen bomb on August 12, 1953.

Today, guided missiles can be launched from their starting points and directed with accuracy at distant targets. The larger explosives are carried by missiles containing the fuel necessary for their propulsion. The gases from this fuel rush with tremendous velocity through a narrow opening. Science is in the process of discovering a fuel which is similar and more efficacious to deal with.

It is said that the Soviet Union already has available rockets with a range up to 600 miles. Soon to come are rockets with a range up to 1,080 miles—if they are not already in use.

It is said that America is attempting to develop rockets with a range of 1,440 miles.

Whether the intercontinental ballistic missile, with its range of 4,800 miles, already exists cannot be ascertained. The Soviet Union has claimed it already has such a missile.

Even without respect to intercontinental ballistic missiles, submarines could launch nuclear attacks on the United States.

The long-range rockets attain unbelievable speed. It is expected that an intercontinental rocket would not take more than twenty minutes to cross the ocean with a payload of nuclear explosive weighing from one to five tons.

How could an atomic war break out today? Not long ago there was talk of local or limited wars that could be contained. But today there is little difference between a local war or a global war. Rocket missiles will be used up to a range of 1,440 miles. The destruction should not be underestimated, even if caused only by a Hiroshima-type bomb.

It can hardly be expected that an enemy will refrain from using atomic bombs or the most devastating hydrogen bombs on large cities at the very outset of a war. One hydrogen bomb now exists that is a thousand times more powerful than the atomic bomb. It will have a destructive radius of many miles. The heat will be 100 million degrees. One can imagine how large would be the number of city-dwellers who would be destroyed by the pressure of the explosion, by flying fragments of glass, by heat and fire and by radio-active waves, even if the attack is only of short duration. The deadly radioactive contamination, as a consequence of the explosion, would have a range of some 45,000 square miles.

An American general has said to some Congressmen: "If at an interval of ten minutes 110 hydrogen bombs are dropped over the U.S.A. there would be a casualty list of about 70 million people; besides, some thousands of square miles would be made useless for a whole generation. Countries like England, West Germany, and France could be finished off with fifteen to twenty hydrogen bombs."

President Eisenhower has pointed out, after watching maneuvers under atomic attack, that defense measures in a future atomic war become useless. In these circumstances all one can do is to pray.

Indeed, not much more can be done in view of an attack by hydrogen bombs than to advise all people living to hide beneath a very strong wall made of stone or cement, and to throw themselves on the ground and to cover the back of their heads, and the body if possible, with cloth. In this way it may be possible to escape annihilation and death through radiation. It is very important that the immediate survivors are given non-radioactive food and drink, and that they be removed immediately from the radioactive district.

It is impossible, however, to erect walls and concrete ceilings of adequate thickness to cover an entire city. Where would the material and the means come from? How would a population have time to run to safety in such bunkers?

In an atomic war there would be neither conqueror nor vanquished. During such a bombardment both sides would suffer the same fate. A continuous destruction would take place and no armistice or peace proposals could bring it to an end.

When people deal with atomic weapons, it is not a matter of superior arms which will decide the issue between them, but only: "Now we want to commit suicide together, destroying each other mutually . . ."

There is a reason for an English M.P. saying: "He who uses atomic weapons becomes subject to the fate of a bee; namely, when it stings it will perish."

Radioactive clouds resulting from a war between East and West would imperil humanity everywhere. There would be no need to use up the remaining stock of atomic and hydrogen bombs, now running literally into the thousands.

A nuclear war is therefore the most senseless and lunatic act that could ever take place. This must be prevented.

When America had its atomic monopoly, it was not necessary to equip its allies with nuclear weapons. Owing to the end of the monopoly, however, this situation is changing. A whole family of nuclear weapons now exists that can be fitted into the military capability of smaller nations.

As a result, the United States is considering a departure from its stated principle not to put atomic weapons into the hands of other countries. If it does so, this could have the gravest consequences. On the other hand, it is comprehensible that the United States wishes to supply the NATO countries with such new weapons for defense against the Soviet Union. The existence of such arms constitutes a new cause of war between the Soviet Union and the U.S., one that did not exist before. Thus, the ground is laid open for nuclear conflict on European soil. The Soviet Union can be reached with long-range rockets from European soil, as far as Moscow and Kharkov, up to 2,400 miles away. Similarly, London, Paris, and Rome are within easy reach of Soviet rocketry.

Rockets of an average range may be used for defense purposes by Turkey and Iran against the Soviet Union. They could penetrate deeply into its country with arms accepted from America.

The Soviet Union is countering those measures. Both America and the Soviet Union may now seek alliances with the Middle East by offering those countries various kinds of financial support. Therefore, events in the Middle East could endanger the peace of the world.

The danger of an atomic war is being increased by the fact that no warning would be given in starting such a war. Indeed, it could erupt merely on the basis of some incident. Thus, the time factor enters—the side that attacks first would have the initial advantage over the attacked. At the very start, the attacked would find himself sustaining losses which would considerably reduce his fighting capacity.

As a result, one has to be on the alert all the time. This factor constitutes an extreme danger in the event of a sudden outbreak of an atomic war. When one has to act with such speed, he has to reckon with the possibility that an error may occur on what is registered on the radar screen, and that this could result in the outbreak of an atomic war.

Attention was drawn to this danger by the American General Curtis LeMay. Quite recently the world found itself in such a situation. The radar station of the American Air Force and American Coastal Command indicated that an invasion of unidentified bombers was on the way. Upon this warning, the general in command of the strategic bomb force ordered that reprisal bombardment should be made. However, realizing that he was taking a great responsibility, he hesitated. Shortly afterward it was pointed out that the radar stations had committed a technical error. What could have happened if a less balanced general had been in his place!

In the future such dangers are likely to increase. Because small rockets exist which pass through the air with terrific speed and are over the target within a few minutes, defense possibilities become very limited. Only seconds remain to identify the markings on the radar screen, so that the counter-attack can spring into being. The theoretical defense consists in sending out missiles to explode the attacking missiles of the enemy before they complete their job, and also in releasing bombers with a view to destroying the ramps from which they are launched.

Such split-second operations cannot be left to the human brain. It works too slowly. The job has therefore been entrusted to an electronic brain.

Such are the heights of our civilization that a cold electronic brain rather than the moral conscience of man may decide human destiny. Are we so certain that an arithmetical or mechanical decision is really superior? The mechanism of the electronic brain may become faulty. It is dependent on the absolute reliability of its complicated functions. Everything has to click to the minutest detail.

Under the circumstances, the greater the number of countries, large or small, that become part of the nuclear arms terror the greater the terror. Naturally, America must assume that the weapons it entrusts to other nations will not be used irresponsibly. But accidents can happen. *Who* can guarantee that there may not be a

"blacksheep" acting on his own, without troubling about the consequences? Who is *able* to keep *all* countries under a situation of rational control? The dam is punctured and it may break down.

That such worries have become very real is shown by the reasoning
of the 9,235 scientists who on January 13 petitioned the United Nations to cease atomic tests. The statement says: "As long as atomic
weapons remain in the hands of the three great powers, agreement
on control is possible. However, if the tests continue and extend to
other countries in possession of atomic weapons, the risks and re-
sponsibilities in regard to an outbreak of an atomic war become
all the greater. From every point of view the danger in a future
atomic war becomes all the more intense, so that an urgent renunciation of atomic weapons becomes absolutely imperative."

America has wisely declared that its objective is to outlaw nuclear weapons. Yet at the same time America seems to be moving
away from the measures necessary to achieve it. America insists that
the missiles it offers to other countries be accepted as quickly as
possible. It wishes to hold such a position as to be able to maintain
peace by nuclear deterrent. It happens, however, that most of the
NATO countries are in no hurry to acquire such weapons because
of an increasingly strengthening public opinion.

In recent months public opinion in Europe has been convinced
that under no circumstances should Europe be allowed to become a
battlefield for an atomic war between the Soviet Union and America.
From this position it will not deviate. The time is past when a European power could plan secretly to establish itself as a big power
by manufacturing atomic weapons exclusively for its own use. In
view of the fact that no public opinion would agree to such an
undertaking, it becomes senseless even to prepare secretly for achieving such a plan.

Gone, too, is the time when NATO generals and European governments can decide on the establishment of launching sites and
stockpiling of atomic weapons. In view of the fact that the dangers
of atomic war and its consequences cannot be avoided, political
procedure as employed hitherto can no longer be considered.

Only agreements that are sanctioned by public opinion are now
valid.

*   *   *

What about the negotiations that could lead to the renunciation of nuclear weapons?

One reads and hears that the success of the projected Summit Conference must depend entirely on its every detail being diplomaically prepared beforehand. The best diplomacy is objectivity. One good way of preparing for a conference (if a respectful and well-meaning criticism is permissible) would be for the statesmen and other representatives to make a change from their present undiplomatic way of dealing with each other and to become diplomatic. Many unnecessary, thoughtless, discourteous, foolish, and offensive remarks have been made by both sides, and this has not been advantageous to the political atmosphere.

It would be fitting if those who have the authority to take the responsibility, and not those who have only nominal authority and who cannot move an inch from their instructions, would confer together.

It would be fitting to go ahead with the conference. For more than five months East and West have talked and written to one another, without any conclusions as to the date and the work program being reached. Public opinion everywhere is finding it difficult to accept this state of affairs and is beginning to ask itself whether a conference which comes into being so limpingly has any hope of really achieving anything.

It would be fitting to hold the conference in a town in some neutral European country, for example, Geneva, as was the case in 1955.

It would be fitting that at this conference only questions that have to do directly with the control and renunciation of nuclear weapons should be discussed.

It would be fitting if not too many people were present at the summit meeting. Only the highest personalities of the three nuclear powers together with their experts and advisers should take their seats there.

Attendance could also be opened on a consultative basis to the representatives of those peoples who—like the NATO countries with

250

America—have connections in nuclear matters; they could then state their opinions on the decisions that hold such grave consequences also for them.

Apart from this, experience teaches us that unnecessarily large attendance brings no advantage to a conference.

The Summit Conference, therefore, is in no way an international or half international one, even though its decisions are of great importance to the whole of mankind.

The three nuclear powers and they alone must decide, in awareness of their repsonsibility to their peoples and to all mankind, whether or not they will renounce the testing and the use of nuclear weapons.

As for planning the conference, impartiality may justify one remark, which is that to date such planning has not been done objectively, and has therefore led nowhere. This leads to the thought that the outcome of a Summit Conference is bound to reflect what went into it.

What is the difference between the partial and the impartial, the fitting and the unfitting in this matter? It lies in the answer to the question on what basis the three nuclear powers decide whether or not to renounce the testing and the use of nuclear weapons.

The unobjective reply would be that the decision will depend on whether an agreement is first reached on comprehensive disarmament or not.

This is a false logic; it presumes that there could be an agreement acceptable to both the East and the West on this issue. But previous negotiations have shown that this is not to be expected; they became stalled right at the start because East and West have been unable to reach agreement even on the conditions under which such discussions should take place.

The anticipated procedure itself is by its very nature not impartial. It is based on false logic. The two vital issues so essential to the very existence of mankind—the cessation of tests and the disposal of nuclear weapons—cannot be made dependent on the Heavens performing the impossible political miracle that alone could insure that none of the three nuclear powers would have any objections to a complete agreement on disarmament.

The fact is that the testing and use of nuclear weapons carry in themselves the absolute reasons for their being renounced. Prior agreement on any other conditions cannot be considered.

Both cause the deepest damage to human rights. The tests do harm to peoples far from the territories of the nuclear powers—endangering their lives and their health—and this in peace time. An atomic war, with its resultant radioactivity, would make the land of peoples not participating in such a war, unlivable. It would be the most unimaginably senseless and cruel way of endangering the existence of mankind. That is why it must not be allowed to happen.

The three nuclear powers owe it to themselves and to mankind to reach agreement on these absolute essentials without first dealing with prior conditions.

The negotiations about disarmament are therefore not the forerunner of such agreement but the outcome of it. They start from the point where agreement on the nuclear issues has been reached, and their goal is to reach the point where the three nuclear powers and the peoples connected with them must agree on guarantees that will seek to avert the danger of a threat of a non-atomic nature taking the place of the previous danger. Everything that the diplomats will have done objectively to prepare the preliminaries to the conference will keep its meaning even if used, not before renunciation, but as the result of it.

Should agreement be reached on the outlawing of nuclear weapons, this by itself will lead to a great improvement in the political situation. As a result of such an agreement, time and distance would again become realities with their own right.

Nuclear weapons, used in conjunction with missiles, change a distant war to a war fought at close range. The Soviet Union and the United States have become next-door neighbors in the modern world but live in constant fear of their lives every minute.

But if nuclear arms should be abolished, the proximity factor would be made less explosive.

Today America has her batteries of nuclear missiles readily available in Europe. Europe has become a connecting land strip between America and Russia, as if the Atlantic had disappeared and the continents had been joined.

But if atomic missiles are outlawed on the basis of effective and enforceable control, this unnatural state of affairs would come to an end. America would again become wholly America; Europe wholly Europe; the Atlantic again wholly the Atlantic Ocean.

The great sacrifices that America brought to Europe during the Second World War and in the years following it will not be forgotten. The many-sided and great help that Europe received from her and the thanks owing for this will not be forgotten.

But the unnatural situation created by the two world wars, which led to a dominating military presence in Europe, cannot continue indefinitely. It must gradually cease to exist—both for the sake of Europe and for the sake of America.

Now there will be shocked voices from all sides: What will become of poor Europe if American atomic weapons no longer defend it from within and from without? Will Europe be delivered to the Soviet? Must it be prepared to languish in a Communist-Babylonian imprisonment for long years?

What Europe and the Europeans have to agree about is that they belong together for better or for worse. This is a new historical fact that can no longer be by-passed politically.

Another factor that must be recognized politically is that it is no longer a question of subjugating peoples, but learning to get along with them intellectually, culturally, spiritually.

A Europe standing on its own has no reason to despair.

Disarmament discussions between the three nuclear powers must seek the guarantees that can bring about actual, total, and durable disposal of nuclear weapons. The question of control and safeguards is a vital one. Reciprocal agreement will have to be reached about allowing international commissions to inspect and investigate on national soil.

One talks of giving aircraft belonging to a world police the right to fly at medium and high altitudes for purposes of aerial inspection.

One asks to what extent a state would be willing to subject itself to such control? It may be said that unfortunate incidents could easily occur as a result. And what about the power that should be entrusted to such a world control? Even the widest form of such control could never insure that everywhere and all the time war could be avoided. But it represents a reasonable basis on which, given time and some relaxation of tension, a workable world system of security might be built.

The same applies also in another matter. As a result of renouncing nuclear arms, the Soviet Union's military might insofar as Europe is concerned would be less affected than that of America. There would remain to the Soviet the many armed divisions with conventional weapons; with those divisions it could easily over-run the NATO states in western Europe—particularly Western Germany—without its being possible for anyone to come to their aid. With this in mind, the Soviet Union should agree in the course of disarmament negotiations to reduce her army, and to commit herself not to undertake steps against Germany. But here, too, no manner of detailed agreements and internationally guaranteed disarmament agreements would be enough. Therefore, we must strive continually to improve the situation, building brick by brick.

We live at a time when the good faith of peoples is doubted more than ever before. Expressions casting doubt on the trustworthiness of the next nation are bandied back and forth. They are based on what happened in the two world wars when the nations experienced dishonesty, injustice, and inhumanity from one another. How can a new trust come about?

We cannot continue in a situation of paralyzing mistrust. If we want to work our way out of the desperate situation in which we find ourselves another spirit must enter into the people. It can come only if the awareness of its necessity suffices to give us strength to believe in its coming. We must presuppose the awareness of this need in all the peoples who have suffered along with us. We must approach them in the spirit that we are human beings, all of us, and that we feel ourselves fitted to feel with each other; to think and to will together in the same way.

The awareness that we are all human beings together has become lost in war and politics. We have reached the point of regarding each other as only members of a people allied with us or against us, and our attitudes, prejudices, sympathies, or antipathies are all conditioned by that fact. Now we must rediscover the fact that we—all together—are human beings, and that we must strive to concede to each other what moral capacity we have.

In that way we can begin to believe that in other peoples too there will arise the need for a new spirit; and that can be the beginning of a feeling of mutual trustworthiness toward each other. The spirit

254

is a mighty force for transforming things. Let us have hope that the spirit can bring people and lands back to an awareness of enlightenment.

At this stage we have the choice of two risks. The one consists in continuing the mad atomic arms race with its danger of unavoidable atomic war in the near future. The other is in the renunciation of nuclear weapons, and the hope that America and the Soviet Union, and the peoples associated with them, will manage to live in peace. The first holds no hope of a prosperous future; the second does. We must risk the second.

In President Eisenhower's speech of November 7, 1957, we find the following: "What the world needs more than a gigantic leap into space is a gigantic leap into peace."

This gigantic leap consists in finding the courage to hope that the spirit of good sense will arise in all peoples and in all lands, a spirit sufficiently strong to overcome the insanity and the inhumanity.

Once agreement on renunciation of nuclear arms has been reached, it would be the responsibility of the United Nations to undertake to see that now, as in the future, they would neither be made nor used. The danger that one or another people might attempt to manufacture nuclear weapons will have to be kept in mind for a long time.

The future holds many difficult problems. The most difficult of these will be the rights of access of over-populated countries to neighboring lands.

But if in our time we renounce nuclear arms, we will have taken the first step on the way to the distant goal of the end to war itself. If we do not do this we remain on the road that leads to atomic war and misery in the near future.

Those who are to meet at the summit must be aware of this, so that they can negotiate with propriety, with the right degree of seriousness, and with a full sense of responsibility.

The Summit Conference must not fail. The will of mankind will not permit it.